CULTURE SMART!
CZECH REPUBLIC

Nicole Rosenleaf Ritter

Graphic Arts Books

First published in Great Britain 2006
by Kuperard, an imprint of Bravo Ltd.

Series Editor Geoffrey Chesler
Design DW Design

Simultaneously published in the U.S.A. and Canada
by Graphic Arts Center Publishing Company
P. O. Box 10306, Portland, OR 97296-0306

Library of Congress Cataloging-in-Publication Data

Ritter, Nicole Rosenleaf.
Czech Republic : a quick guide to customs and etiquette /
Nicole Rosenleaf Ritter.
      p. cm. — (Culture smart!)
Includes bibliographical references and index.
ISBN 1-55868-917-6 (softbound : alk. paper)
1. Czech Republic—Social life and customs. 2. Etiquette—Czech Republic.
3. National characteristics, Czech. I. Title. II. Series.
DB2035.R58 2005
943.71—dc22

                                    2005019451

Printed in Malaysia

Cover image: The Round Tower, Český Krumlov, Bohemia.
Travel Ink/Lee Corbett

About the Author

NICOLE ROSENLEAF RITTER is a writer and editor specializing in the post-Communist countries of Central and Eastern Europe, the Balkans, and the former Soviet Union. After earning an MA from Yale University in Russian and East European Studies in 1998 and then working for international travel and life icon *Transitions Abroad* magazine, Nicole moved to the Czech Republic with her husband. She lived and worked in Prague—primarily as an editor for the Internet magazine and journalism training nonprofit *Transitions Online*—for more than four years, moving back to her home state of Montana in 2004 with her family.

Other Books in the Series

- Culture Smart! Argentina
- Culture Smart! Australia
- Culture Smart! Belgium
- Culture Smart! Brazil
- Culture Smart! Britain
- Culture Smart! Costa Rica
- Culture Smart! China
- Culture Smart! Denmark
- Culture Smart! Finland
- Culture Smart! France
- Culture Smart! Germany
- Culture Smart! Greece
- Culture Smart! Hong Kong
- Culture Smart! India
- Culture Smart! Ireland
- Culture Smart! Italy
- Culture Smart! Japan
- Culture Smart! Korea
- Culture Smart! Mexico
- Culture Smart! Netherlands
- Culture Smart! Czech Republic
- Culture Smart! Philippines
- Culture Smart! Poland
- Culture Smart! Portugal
- Culture Smart! Russia
- Culture Smart! Singapore
- Culture Smart! Spain
- Culture Smart! Sweden
- Culture Smart! Switzerland
- Culture Smart! Thailand
- Culture Smart! Turkey
- Culture Smart! Ukraine
- Culture Smart! USA
- Culture Smart! Vietnam

Other titles are in preparation. For more information, contact: info@kuperard.co.uk

The publishers would like to thank **CultureSmart!**Consulting for its help in researching and developing the concept for this series.

CultureSmart!Consulting creates tailor-made seminars and consultancy programs to meet a wide range of corporate, public-sector, and individual needs. Whether delivering courses on multicultural team building in the U.S.A., preparing Chinese engineers for a posting in Europe, training call-center staff in India, or raising the awareness of police forces to the needs of diverse ethnic communities, we provide essential, practical, and powerful skills worldwide to an increasingly international workforce.

For details, visit www.culturesmartconsulting.com

contents

contents

Map of the Czech Republic

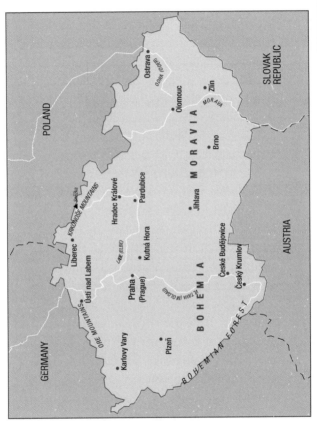

introduction

This Culture Smart! guide to the Czech Republic is designed to give you some insight into the humanity of the Czech people. Since the fall of Communism in 1989, millions of tourists have touched down at Prague airport with the hope of finding some of the magic described to them in the countless articles written about the Czech capital since it opened up. How many left with insight into the culture is impossible to say.

The sad fact is that many tourists visit the Czech Republic knowing no more about it than that beer is cheap and the women are beautiful. That lack of knowledge has led to frustration among Czechs, most of whom are well-educated and informed about the world around them, and who sometimes view all tourists as cut from the same cloth.

Czechs value knowledge and cultivation, sometimes to the point of seeming snobbish. That intellectual ambition cuts across class lines, so it is never safe to assume that you can tell someone's status from their appearance. Czechs also value formality and hierarchy, which can make them seem stiff, distant, or even unfriendly—certainly a few bad encounters with service workers and bureaucrats could sour a visitor's impression.

But beneath the layers of social reserve, Czechs

are a deeply sincere and caring people. It's a side most visitors never get to see unless they are alert to it, but it is visible every time a surly looking teenager gets up to give his streetcar seat to an elderly lady or a middle-aged man stops to coo at a baby in a carriage. Those fortunate enough to make friends with Czechs see it in the fierce loyalty they have for their intimates. Once a Czech calls someone a friend—and it won't happen overnight—that friendship can last forever.

The Czechs are also deeply, blackly funny, with a distinctive, many-layered sense of humor. They are a people who have made laughing through tears a national survival strategy.

This book introduces you to the customs, values, and attitudes of a remarkable people, and the role of history in shaping these. It describes Czech life at home and in the workplace, and offers practical advice on what to expect and how to behave in unfamiliar social situations.

Visiting the Czech Republic will always be worthwhile—its incredible sights are enough to satisfy any aesthete's need for beauty. But the real rewards will come for the visitor who cares enough to try to get inside the culture, beyond the reserve to the complex corners of the Czech soul.

Key Facts

Official Name	Czech Republic (*Česká republika*)	Founded on January 1, 1993, when Czechoslovakia split into the Czech Republic and Slovakia
Capital City	Prague (Praha)	Population 1.2 million
Other Major Cities	Brno (capital of Moravia) 376,400 population	Ostrava, Plzeň, Olomouc
Area	30,450 sq. miles (78,866 sq. km.)	Slightly smaller than South Carolina
Borders	Germany, Slovakia, Poland, Austria	Shares longest border with Poland
Climate	Generally mild with few extremes. Four distinct seasons, all featuring considerable rain.	Summers can be warm and humid but also cool and rainy. Winters tend to be cool and overcast.
Currency	Czech crown (*koruna*)	Crown divided into 100 *hellers*.
Population	10.2 million	Has one of the lowest birthrates in the world
Ethnic Makeup	81% Czech, 13% Moravian, 6% other	Minorities include Slovaks, Roma (Gypsies), Poles, Germans, and Hungarians.
Language	Czech	Slavic language
Religion	65% without religion, 27% Catholic, 5% Protestant, 3% Orthodox	Has one of the highest rates of atheism in the world.

Government	Parliamentary democracy	President elected by parliament.
Media	Main national newspapers are *Mladá fronta Dnes*, *Lidové noviny*, *Hospodářské noviny*, and *Právo*.	Media is largely free of government interference.
Media: English Language	The *Prague Post* (weekly newspaper). Radio Prague English-language daily news. BBC World Service. Additional international channels available on cable and satellite television/radio	Foreign-language print media is widely available in the capital. Most hotels have satellite or cable television.
Electricity	220 volts and a standard two-prong plug	U.S. appliances require adapters/converters.
Video/TV	PAL B/G (cable), PAL D/K (broadcast)	NTSC format (used in the U.S.) will not work
Telephone	Country code is 420; Prague city code is 2	To dial a U.S. number, use 001+area code and number
Time Zones	Central European Time	2 hours ahead of GMT and 6 hours ahead of New York

chapter one

LAND &
PEOPLE

Glinting spires, winding cobblestone lanes, mountaintop castles, and red roofs as far as the eye can see—how could anyone fail to be charmed by this most charming of Central European countries? Trapped behind the Iron Curtain for more than forty years, Czechoslovakia burst its bounds in 1989 and emerged as a must-see destination for anyone pining for a perfectly preserved piece of scenic paradise.

By the time Czechoslovakia split into the Czech Republic and Slovakia in 1993, the Czech Republic—and especially Prague—was already starting to find a place "on the traveling map," due to its reasonable prices, beautiful panoramas, and uniquely "Bohemian" flavor.

More than ten years on, the Czech Republic may no longer be considered an exotic destination, but it is one with considerable magic left for visitors. From Prague's Old Town—Europe's only historical center almost completely untouched by the Second World War—to its castle, and from Český Krumlov's tiny

Renaissance glory to Karlovy Vary's old-world
spa town ambience, there is enough beauty and
atmosphere to intrigue even the most jaded visitor.

GEOGRAPHY

Slightly smaller than South Carolina, the Czech
Republic is a landlocked, temperate country that
borders Germany, Slovakia, Poland, and Austria.
One of the world's newest independent states, the
Czech Republic was founded on January 1, 1993,
after the breakup of Czechoslovakia, a state first
recognized in 1918.

Today's Czech Republic consists of two
primary historical areas, Bohemia (*Čechy*) in the
west and Moravia (*Morava*) in the east. The
Bohemian landscape is characterized by hills and
gently rolling plains flanked by low mountains,
while Moravia has a slightly more mountainous
terrain. Important rivers include the Labe (Elbe),

Vltava (Moldau), Morava, and Odra (Oder). Slovakia ended up with most of the mountains in the split, but the Czech Republic still boasts several high peaks in the Krkonoše (Giant) mountain range, including Sněžka at 5,200 feet (1,600 meters) above sea level.

The capital city, Prague, is also considered to be the historical capital of the Czech people and is now home to approximately 1.2 million people. The Moravian first city, Brno, is also the second-largest city in the Czech Republic with a population of approximately 370,000. Ethnic Czechs comprise some 81 percent of the Czech population of approximately 10 million, while ethnic Moravians—who do not speak a separate language, although some would contend they speak more proper Czech—make up approximately 13 percent of the country's people. Other ethnic groups include Slovaks, Poles, Germans, Hungarians, and Roma, also known as Gypsies.

Politically, the country is now divided into thirteen regions, called *kraj* (the plural is *kraje*)

and its capital city, Prague. Besides Prague and Brno, the only other city with a population of over 300,000 is the Moravian city of Ostrava. Neither Brno nor Ostrava is as well-known internationally as two smaller cities, however: Plzeň and České Budějovice, while perhaps not recognizable by name, are internationally known for two of the Czech Republic's most famous exports, Pilsner Urquell and Budvar (Budweiser) beers. (The latter brand has been locked in an international struggle with U.S. beer giant Anheuser-Busch for trademark rights to the "Budweiser" name.)

After Prague, the most common tourist destinations are medieval silver town Kutná Hora, UNESCO heritage site Český Krumlov, and the spa towns of western Bohemia.

The Czech Republic's location and geography have lent it a temperate climate, with humid, warm summers; short, mild springs and falls; and rainy, cold, and very gray winters. As a guideline, the average temperature in Prague ranges from 22°F (-5°C) to 33°F (0°C) in January and from 53°F (12°C) to 74°F (23°C) in July.

As the temperate climate would suggest, there are few extremes in Czech weather, although the precipitation levels combined with the low-lying terrain can lead to widespread and extremely damaging floods, as happened in 2002.

A BRIEF HISTORY

The oldest recorded settlers in the present-day Czech Republic were a Celtic tribe called the Boii, from which the name Bohemia stems (from the Latin *Boiohaemum*). The Boii lived in the region starting from the fourth century BCE and were eventually joined by Germanic tribes.

Slavic peoples ventured into the territories of present-day Moravia and Slovakia in the sixth century CE. In the ninth century the kingdom of Greater Moravia, in the eastern part of the region, was founded by the Slavic prince Sviatopluk, and Christianity was adopted. In 906 Moravia was conquered by Magyars. In around 995 the state of Bohemia in the northwest broke away from Moravia under the homegrown Přemyslid dynasty. This dynasty, which ruled the Czech lands until 1306, has its roots in the semilegendary Princess Libuše, sometimes called the Mother of the Czech Nation. According to the most famous telling of the legend, written in the height of the nineteenth-century Czech national revival by Alois Jirásek, Libuše foretold the founding of Prague standing on the hill at Vyšehrad by saying, "Behold, I see a great city, whose fame will touch the stars."

Princess Libuše ruled the Czech lands wisely, and her people were happy, as Jirásek tells it, until two men quarreling over land questioned her judgment because she was a woman. Incensed, she chastised them for not appreciating her sensitive ruling style and told them to find her a husband who could rule in her place. She even told them where to find him and what he would be—a simple plowman (*Přemysl*). When they returned with Přemysl, the two were wed, thus founding the Přemyslid dynasty.

In around 880, the first Přemyslid prince, Bořivoj, founded Prague Castle high above the Vltava River, transferring power there from the fortress of Vyšehrad. During the Přemyslid reign, the Czech state managed to maintain titular sovereignty, despite its incorporation into the Holy Roman Empire in 950 CE. The assassination of the pious Prince Wenceslas (Václav) by his pagan brother Boleslav in 935 created a Christian martyr and a symbol of Czech nationalism, and Wenceslas became the patron saint of Bohemia.

The Kingdom of Bohemia

In 1029 Moravia became a fief of Bohemia, and in the twelfth century Bohemia became a kingdom. Under Otakar II, who reigned from 1253 to 1278, the Czech kingdom expanded to include territory in modern-day Austria and Slovenia. The

Přemyslid dynasty died out after the murder of Wenceslas III, but the Czech lands experienced a high point in power and prestige under Charles IV (of the Luxembourg ruling family, who had married into the Přesmyslids in the early fourteenth century), who reigned from 1346 to 1378. Charles IV was elected Holy Roman Emperor in 1355 and founded a number of notable institutions, including Charles University, the oldest university in central Europe.

The Hussite Wars

In the fifteenth century, a homegrown precursor of the Protestant Reformation—a movement called the Hussites, after its leader Jan Hus—swept the nation and alarmed the papacy. Hus was tried by the Council of Constance for heresy and burned at the stake in 1415, but his ideas lived on. The anger aroused by this act led to the  Hussite Wars (1420–36), in which the reformist armies led by Jan Žižka held the Catholic Emperor's superior forces at bay. By the mid-fifteenth century, the Catholic Church and the Hussites had reached an uneasy truce that allowed the largely Protestant Czech nobility to gain in strength, but by 1526, the Austrian-Catholic Habsburgs had taken control of Bohemia.

Habsburg Rule

That control was cemented in 1620 with the defeat of the Bohemian nobility at the Battle of White Mountain, in part precipitating the Thirty Years' War. (The "defenestration" in 1618 of three royal Catholic officials from the Old Royal Palace of Prague Castle hadn't helped relations much either.) Following their defeat at White Mountain—an event still commemorated by a monument on Old Town Square—Czechs were forced to convert to Catholicism or leave, a policy that has perhaps led to the Czech objection to organized religion even today. Leading the fight against Protestantism were the Jesuits, who built many new churches in the Baroque style.

The Czech lands remained part of the Habsburg empire—and were subject to its attendant assimilation and Germanization policies—until 1918. By the nineteenth century, the Czech language itself was in danger of dying out, with the educated classes speaking and writing German. In 1848, a national revival of language and culture turned political, and the Czechs began demanding greater sovereignty. With the creation of the dual Austro-Hungarian monarchy in 1867, Bohemia was reduced to a province of Austria, and nationalist sentiment grew. But the goal of an independent state would not be reached until after the First World War, when the empire dissolved following Austria-Hungary's defeat in the war.

Independence

The postwar Treaty of Versailles enshrined the principle of national self-determination, and on October 28, 1918, the sovereign state of Czechoslovakia was founded.

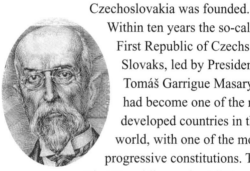

Within ten years the so-called First Republic of Czechs and Slovaks, led by President Tomáš Garrigue Masaryk, had become one of the most developed countries in the world, with one of the most progressive constitutions. The First Republic survived little more than twenty years, however, with the Munich Conference ceding control of the northern Sudetenland districts, which were home to many ethnic Germans, to Nazi Germany in the infamous policy of appeasement. The remainder of Czechoslovakia was annexed by Germany in 1939. President Eduard Beneš set up a government-in-exile in London. The Nazi occupation lasted from March 1939 through the end of the Second World War in May 1945.

The Nazi Occupation

After Czechoslovakia was liberated by Soviet and American troops in 1945, a government of national unity was formed under Beneš. The country expelled its two to three million ethnic German citizens, and thousands were killed in the process. The expulsion increased ill relations between Czechoslovakia and its neighbors, Germany and Austria, and groups of expellees living outside Czech territory are still lobbying for compensation for lost property. However, most Czechs believe the expulsions were justified because of the suffering experienced under Nazi occupation—suffering that included not only brutal repression of Czechs in the Protectorate of Bohemia and Moravia but also the deportation and extermination of most of the Gypsies (Roma) and Jews living in the country.

One of the most notorious events that occurred in the Protectorate during the war was the assassination of Reinhard Heydrich, the deputy Reich Protector of Bohemia and Moravia, who ruled the lands with an iron fist. In 1942, a group of Czech resistance fighters who had been trained in England were returned to Prague to carry out an assassination. Although Heydrich was only wounded in the daring attack, he died a week later of blood poisoning brought about by the shrapnel lodged in his wounds.

As retaliation for the death of Heydrich, German Gestapo and SS killed as many as 1,000 Czechs suspected of being involved in the assassination and deported 3,000 Jews. But the reprisals did not stop there. In June, just days after Heydrich died, Hitler commanded that the small Czech town of Lidice be liquidated for its role in helping the assassins—a charge that had no basis in fact. Nearly 200 men and boys over the age of sixteen were shot, while the women were sent to a concentration camp. Young children were sent to another camp. The village was then completely razed, destroyed house by house, and crops were planted over the area.

In addition to dramatic events such as these, ordinary Czechs were deported to serve as slave labor in German factories and Gestapo roundups, arbitrary violence and executions, and near-starvation conditions were everyday occurrences.

Stalinism

Following the war, by the terms of the deal struck at Yalta, Czechoslovakia was placed into the formal Soviet sphere of influence, and a February 1948 takeover by the Communists forced the young country behind the Iron Curtain to suffer more indignities as an occupied country. Stalinist show trials in the 1950s—set up to purge the Czechoslovak Communist Party of those who were not considered sufficiently supportive of Stalinism—terrorized the populace and led most people to retreat into themselves.

The Prague Spring

In the late 1960s, Czech Communists led by Alexander Dubček did attempt to lighten the hand of the regime in a reform effort christened the Prague Spring, but the August 1968 invasion by the armies of the Warsaw Pact ended the experiment of "Socialism With a Human Face." In 1977 a human rights group of intellectuals called "Charter 77," which included the playwright Václav Havel, was formed. This led to a crackdown against dissidents.

The Velvet Revolution

Czechoslovakia languished under Communist rule until 1989, until the decay of the Soviet empire and the decline of the Communist system led to unrest and demonstrations around Eastern and Central Europe, culminating in Czechoslovakia in the November '89 demonstrations—under the spiritual guidance of Alexander Dubček and Václav Havel—that led to the fall of the Communist regime. New political parties were formed and legalized, and the Communist Party was stripped of its powers. Havel was appointed president and amnesty was granted to thousands of prisoners. The events were popularly known as the Velvet Revolution.

The Parting of the Ways

Political wrangling between politicians in Czechoslovakia's two ethnic constituencies— most notably former Slovak Prime Minister Vladimir Mečiar and former Czech Prime Minister (now president) Václav Klaus—led to a parliamentary decision to split the country into the Czech Republic and Slovakia (sometimes called the Velvet Divorce). A referendum on the issue was never held, but the country was split on January 1, 1993, and Václav Havel elected the president of the Czech Republic. At the time, polls indicated that only 9 percent of the population supported the break, although polls taken on the tenth anniversary of the split showed that people in both countries were now glad to have their separate republics.

Since 1993, the Czech Republic has been successful in integrating into wider multinational structures, including NATO in 1999 and the European Union in 2004.

THE CZECH GOVERNMENT

The Czech Republic is a parliamentary democracy. The country's main political parties include the leftist Czech Social Democratic Party (ČSSD) and the rightist Civic Democratic Party (ODS)—who have swapped primary power back and forth since independence—and the Christian and Democratic Union-Czechoslovak People's

Party (KDU-ČSL), the Freedom Union-Democratic Union (US-DEU), and the Communist Party of Bohemia and Moravia (KSČM).

The president is not directly elected but is instead chosen by the parliament for a five-year term. President Havel stepped down after ten years in power in the winter of 2003 and was ultimately replaced by former prime minister, ODS leader, and Havel rival Václav Klaus after several contentious rounds of elections.

Political participation by Czech citizens has waned since the early heyday of the flowering of democracy following the overthrow of Communism. Cynicism and apathy have taken their toll on the democratic process, but overall the government and citizenry remain committed to democracy and European-style capitalism.

THE CZECH ECONOMY

Czechoslovakia under Communism had a great
many industrial areas and manufacturing plants,
as well as some mining. Much of the heavy
industry was located in Slovakia, meaning that
after the 1993 split, the Czech Republic was left
without that decaying industrial legacy, but for a
few spots in Northern Bohemia. The Czech
Republic has prospered since then, becoming one
of the stars of the post-Communist region, but for
a recession shortly before 2000 that ended
relatively quickly.

Today, the Czech economy is diversified. The
main manufacturing industries, according to the
Czech Foreign Ministry, are machines, transport
equipment, power, glass, jewelry, porcelain,
chemicals and pharmaceuticals, steel
and iron, textiles and clothing,
aerospace, food processing, and
brewing, as well as agriculture in
grain, potatoes, sugar beets,
oilseeds, fruits, vegetables,
livestock, and milk.

The largest sector of the economy is
services—including such industries as
telecommunications, banking, and education—
which make up approximately 60 percent of GDP.
Tourism also plays a large role. Industry accounts
for 35 percent, and some Czech products—such

as Škoda cars (now owned by Volkswagen), Pilsner beer, and Czech-made streetcars and trolleys (used in cities worldwide including Portland, Oregon)—are internationally famous. Agriculture still plays a small but important part in the economy, approximately 5 percent of GDP.

The country's currency, the Czech crown (*koruna*) (CZK), has had a run of strength against the dollar and euro in the last two years and looks set to continue to appreciate against the weakening dollar. Inflation is low, but the country's deficits and stubborn 9 to 10 percent unemployment rate remain a concern. The Czech government has also had trouble completing deals for privatization of the country's large state-owned monopolies, including ČEZ, the energy giant, and the telecommunications company Český Telecom.

In Prague and other selected, highly visited pockets such as Český Krumlov and Karlovy Vary, much of the economy is based on tourism, with fluctuations in tourist numbers causing much anxiety among the many people who are dependent on tourist dollars. The Czech tourism industry took a heavy hit in 2002 when the worst floods in one hundred years—maybe as many as 1,000 years—hit the country and especially the capital. Visitor numbers have returned since then, but that year is remembered as a black one for one of the country's leading industries.

There has been heavy investment in the tourist industry in many of these areas by foreigners, especially Russians, and many Czechs resent that presence. Karlovy Vary—a small, historic spa town in western Bohemia still sometimes known by its German name, Karlsbad—in particular has become so popular among the Russian *nouveaux riches* that there is a direct Czech Air flight between the town of 50,000 and the Russian capital of Moscow.

Prague has also become a popular choice for international company and organization headquarters in Central Europe. German shipping giant DHL recently moved its IT headquarters to Prague, and Radio Free Europe/Radio Liberty is still headquartered (for now) in downtown Prague.

CZECHS AROUND THE WORLD
Immigrants from the Czech lands can be found around the world, with high concentrations in the Midwestern United States and in the U.S. state of Texas dating from the nineteenth and early in the twentieth century. (There is even a National Czech and Slovak Museum and Library in Iowa!)

During the Communist era—and especially

after 1968—large numbers of dissidents fled the country for points abroad, including the United States, Canada, Australia, and other "Western" countries. After the fall of Communism, many of these émigrés returned to their former homeland.

Czechs today continue to emigrate, but not in the numbers once seen. There is, however, a steady stream of human "exports" in the form of top-level athletes, especially hockey and football (soccer) players, with Czechs reaching the apex of international and European competition. Some of the best-known modern Czechs are athletes, including tennis star Martina Navratilova (who became an American citizen after defecting in 1975 but was born in Prague) and National Hockey League goalie Dominik Hasek (nicknamed "The Dominator").

The Czech lands throughout history have produced a tremendous number of famous and important cultural figures as well. Well-known writers of Czech origin include Franz Kafka (*The Trial*, *Metamorphosis*), Karel Čapek (inventor of the word "robot"), and Milan Kundera (*The Unbearable Lightness of Being*). Antonin Dvořák, Bedřich Smetana, Leoš Janáček, and Bohuslav

Martinů represent the most famous Czech composers, although other classical giants, including W. A. Mozart, also worked and lived in Prague at various periods in their lives.

Film is another genre in which Czechs have made impressive contributions. Miloš Forman (*Amadeus*, *One Flew Over the Cuckoo's Nest*), Jiří Menzel (1967 Academy Award winner, *Closely Watched Trains*), and animator and short filmmaker Jan Švankmajer are all Czechs who have achieved the highest levels in their art. Famous Czech visual artists include Art Nouveau giant Alfons Mucha, whose images are immediately recognizable in posters adorning all manner of Czech establishments.

The Czechs have also produced some of the modern era's best-known philosophers and statesmen—by happy coincidence, sometimes in the same person—including post-Communist Czech president and playwright Václav Havel and philosopher and first president of Czechoslovakia, Tomáš Garrigue Masaryk, who espoused such radical notions as equality for women in the early twentieth century.

Well before the nineteenth and twentieth centuries, Czechs were also known for porcelain, ceramics, and especially hand-cut lead crystal. The Czech contribution to architecture is on display at its best in Prague, where Gothic castle remains mingle with the height of Art Nouveau. Prague is also home to one of the only examples of Cubist architecture, the House of the Black Madonna, which now houses the Museum of Czech Cubism.

The sum total of Czech contributions to world culture is impossible to measure but is certainly impressive by any standard, especially given the country's small size and history of oppression by outside forces. It's a tradition of which Czechs are justifiably proud and that modern Czechs show every sign of continuing.

chapter two

VALUES & ATTITUDES

We are a small nation. We were never the conquerors but rather the victims. Before the Second World War we concentrated on Great Britain and France. Then there was the Munich Agreement and we lost. Then we concentrated on the Soviet Union, the great Slavic brother, and we were occupied in 1968. So, this is deeply rooted in the generations . . . a kind of genetic information that's been given and that will have some influence in some period of time.

Professor Vladmira Dvořákova, in "Czech National Identity," a Radio Prague broadcast, October 28, 2003.

It is impossible to sum up any culture in just a few words, but if it came down to finding three adjectives to describe Czechs as a whole, those three would be resilient, reserved, and clever.

RESILIENCE

To look at Czech history and the Czech nation is to see a living embodiment of resilience. In the past hundred years alone, the Czech Republic has gone from imperial possession, to independent nation united with the Slovaks, to Nazi-occupied "protectorate," to Soviet bloc state, to independent, post-Communist nation united with the Slovaks, to fully fledged independent state and E.U. member. To say a lot has happened to Czechs and the Czech nation in only a century would be a gross understatement.

Such upheavals have left a people able to survive seemingly anything—from Soviet invasions to surly wait staff—and do so with a bare minimum of whining. With great changes comes great perspective, to twist the Spiderman maxim, and Czech people have perspective about what is important in spades.

Here's one example. The Náměstí Míru metro station has an escalator that is nearly a third of a kilometer long (1,094 feet). It is the longest, steepest escalator in all the Czech Republic, and when it breaks down, the whole station closes. Anyone unlucky enough not to hear or understand the closure notice from the inside of the metro car must climb to the top of the escalator's many double-long stairs or wait the possible hours until it can be fixed.

On one occasion, an eighty-two-year-old woman was stuck at the bottom. Without complaining, or demanding help, she simply grabbed her purse firmly and began to climb. She climbed at the same steady rate, not slowing down or speeding up, until she reached the top, at which point she loosened the grip on her handbag and headed for the exit stairs to the outside. Some Americans, who had also been stuck, may have reached the top first, but they were powered by whining and drama. For the Czech *babička* (grandmother) a broken, extra-long escalator was just another day at the office—nothing at all compared to the collapse of nations, occupation of foreign powers, or Soviet tank invasion.

RESERVE

It is the reserved nature of Czechs that visitors may notice first, however. Emotion in speech is hard to gauge as Czechs speak in low tones and with a minimum of inflection. Smiles come only with good reason and almost always for friends, not strangers (see also page 158). Modern Czechs have perfected what can only be described as a bland facade—a sort of facial shrug of "whatever"—in dealing with strangers. Neither offensive nor friendly, the utter lack of visible emotion can be infuriating for someone who *is* feeling strongly after a poor service encounter or particularly trying bureaucratic moment, for example.

One way to demonstrate the reserve of Czechs is to look at a linguistic tradition. The way to inquire about how someone is doing—the Czech equivalent of "How are you?"—is to ask *"Jak se máš/máte?"* (The first is used with close friends or other intimates, the second with acquaintances, superiors, or strangers. There is more about Czech forms of greeting in Chapter 9.) It literally means "How do you have yourself?"

In American or British English, of course, the normal answer is "fine," but there are almost countless acceptable ways to answer it, ranging from "horrible" to "excellent." In Czech, it is of course possible to express all those sentiments grammatically, but the rule is that no one is ever having themselves *dobře* (well), much less *skvěle* (excellently). To express such strong emotion—especially positive—would almost seem like bragging. The neutral, accepted answer to the question is *"Jde to,"* which literally means "It's going" but is closer in actual meaning to the plain, boring "fine."

CLEVERNESS

Czech cleverness, meanwhile, manifests itself in a number of different ways. It is clear to anyone who gets to know Czechs well—and especially if that visitor or foreigner can speak or understand Czech—that most are well-read and well-educated. There is a basic level of education and literacy that cuts across most generational and even many class lines. More so than erudition, however, the Czech intellect comes out in its humor—black, witty, and subversive.

The Czech sense of intelligent humor and how it helps them to cope with their lot in life in a small country prone to invasion and occupation can be best illustrated by the twentieth-century Czech literary classic *The Good Soldier Švejk*, written by Jarošlav Hasek in 1915 after he had been drafted to serve in the Austro-Hungarian forces in the First World War. The character of Švejk—who is taken by his superiors to be a lazy dullard but who ultimately exposes the hypocrisies and inadequacies of the empire in which he is forced to serve—is the basis for the term "Švejkism," which is sometimes used to describe an element of Czech character: "to survive in the face of adversity and absurd situations," to quote Radio Prague.

Švejk, despite hardships and lowly status, always comes out on top, using "crazy like a fox" methods of passive resistance. Švejkism has in fact become a sort of shorthand for the Czech's peculiar talent for passive resistance, a trait with which some Czechs would rather not be associated. As *Švejk* translator Cecil Parrott wrote in an introduction to his English version of the novel quoted by Radio Prague, "There were many

Czechs who thought then [during the First Republic, when the book was first published] and still do now that Švejk himself is not a good advertisement for the Czech character." Švejkism is therefore not a neutral way to describe Czechs, even though a great many will admit that the character of Švejk and the cleverness of his resistance has become almost universally associated with the Czech psyche.

NENÍ MOŽNÉ

The combination of these three characteristics—cleverness, reserve, and resilience—along with generations of first Austro-Hungarian and then Communist bureaucracy has also led to a particular form of passive resistance, an attitude that some foreigners can characterize only using the Czech phrase they associate with it: *Není možné*. Literally meaning "It isn't possible," *Není možné* is a catch-all for uncooperative retail workers who don't want to accept a return, postal clerks who won't help someone who stood in the "wrong" line, and wait staff who don't think that *guláš* can be served with anything other than dumplings.

Coming from cultures in which the customer is always right and complaining to higher-ups is a form of currency that can be used to improve treatment, some visitors will find *Není možné* hard to swallow. Delivered as it usually is with a bland demeanor, *Není možné* is seldom the final word, if you're willing to argue long and hard enough, in Czech if possible. But if you can't express yourself in Czech, don't be surprised if a Czech friend refuses to do such heavy lifting. When faced with a *Není možné*, most Czechs will simply accept it and move on. Unless it's a matter of life and death, most visitors would be well-advised to do the same for the sake of their sanity.

ATTITUDES TOWARD FOREIGNERS AND VISIBLE MINORITIES

The Czech Republic is a fairly homogenous place—before 1945, most people had never met a person of African descent, for example—and until 1989, it was also not a common tourist destination. Given that, it is perhaps not surprising that attitudes toward foreigners—and in particular toward visible minorities and people of color— have been slow to change. Most of the time this mild xenophobia expresses itself in little more than stares and rude comments (usually in Czech, because most Czechs assume foreigners will not bother to learn the language), but incidents of racial violence and skinhead activity have also been on the rise since the fall of Communism.

For visible minorities, the Czech Republic can

sometimes be an uncomfortable place because political correctness has not filtered down to street level. At soccer matches, fans have been known to make monkey noises and throw bananas at black players. Older people on the metro will sometimes stare openly at people of color (even more than they would normally stare), and Asians are stereotyped as purveyors of poor-quality goods and often spoken of derisively. (Prague has a large Vietnamese community as a result of Communist-era treaties, and many of these immigrants own small shops.)

Still, it is the Czech Republic's largest homegrown visible minority group—the Roma, or Gypsies—that is the target of the harshest treatment. Many Czechs, even highly educated people, say plainly that they don't consider themselves to be bigoted but that they simply don't like Roma and don't even consider them to be Czech. That hostility stems in part from the Roma's lack of integration into larger society— many people did not attend school with Roma or do not now work with Romani people because of social stratification—and from the perception of the Roma community as being a hotbed of criminal activity. It is true that some Roma support themselves and their families with petty crime such as shoplifting, and that certainly doesn't help matters.

Visitors who resemble people of Romani ethnicity—chiefly South Asians, since ethnic Roma are believed to have originated in India—may find that they receive especially hostile treatment in the Czech Republic. Once observed speaking English, that treatment may improve slightly.

In Prague in particular, foreign tourists of all colors have become a constant, almost year-round presence. By now, most Czechs simply avoid tourist spots or confine their complaints to low-voiced expressions of irritation. Visitors who want to avoid being the target of such volleys can try to limit the "cultural impact" of their visit (by reading this book, for example), but there may still be people who resent their presence. It's best not to take it personally and remember that Czechs are still pretty sensitive about foreign invasions, even when they are of the tourist variety. Such attitudes are likely to change as the next generation of Czechs becomes more racially and culturally diverse—and especially now that the Czech Republic is a member of the European Union.

ATTITUDES TOWARD WOMEN

Some visitors may also find a few typical Czech beliefs about women hard to take, although that too is changing slowly. During the Communist era, women were "granted" Soviet-style equality, which meant that women were supposed to be eligible for all the same educational and vocational possibilities as men, and all women were required to work. While women in this era did see an opening of vistas in career paths, societal expectations toward home roles changed little. Women were still expected to be the primary caretaker of home and children, even when they were working as many hours as men were.

What "equality" meant for women, especially mothers with children, was little more than perpetual exhaustion. Men refused to help out around the house—preferring instead to go to the pub in the evening or watch television—and so women were stuck working both in and out of the home. As a result, the idea of "feminism" got a bad rap in the Czech Republic, one that it hasn't managed to shake.

In the post-Communist Czech Republic, women are freer to decide whether to stay home with their children or to work full-time outside the home, but many Czechs—even women—still associate feminism with being forced to work the equivalent of two full-time jobs.

In the workplace, males still control the upper echelons of most professions (with the notable exception of medicine), and women are often consigned to administrative positions. Sexual harassment is certainly an issue, although it is not widely recognized as problematic—many see the entire concept, along with the idea of sexism in general, as an unwanted Western import—and workplaces can seem quite male-dominated, especially to foreigners.

Young women and women with children in particular often have trouble finding good jobs because of a perception that they will get pregnant and want to take endless maternity leave or that their children will require too much of their time. And it is still perfectly legal and acceptable to advertise a job only to men—or, sometimes, to attractive young women. (Czechs do not enjoy preemployment privacy protection and may be asked about their age, marital status, family plans, and all manner of other things an American employer would risk stiff fines asking.)

Visitors to the Czech Republic may also be surprised at the prevalence of the sex trade in Prague and in border regions. Such establishments are usually accompanied by quite graphic advertising, and nudity in general is tolerated in ads for products ranging from bottled water to hand soap.

As in attitudes toward foreigners and minorities, beliefs about a woman's "place" are changing, but it is a slow process. For good or for bad, few Czechs feel the need to sugarcoat what may strike some as controversial and/or even sexist language. Feminism is still seen largely as something for Western women, and that idea doesn't seem to be going anywhere fast.

HIERARCHY AND TITLES

Despite four decades of a "classless society" under Communism, titles and hierarchy remain important social indicators in Czech modern life. By and large, these are based on academic achievement. The Austro-Hungarian bureaucracy was enamored of titles, and that love continues even into the modern Czech Republic, with all business cards sporting the one or more titles that most professionals hold and even mailbox labels showing evidence of academic and professional distinction.

The most common titles are *inženýr* (Ing.), which indicates a university degree in sciences, and *magistr* (Mgr.), which is roughly equivalent to a master's degree. Other possible titles that one is likely to come across include PhDr. (*doktor*, holding a doctorate), JUDr. (*doktor,* law degree), MUDr. (*doktor*, medical degree), and Prof. (professor, holding a doctorate and professorship).

In referring to someone with a title, it is proper in Czech to use both Mr. and Ms./Mrs. plus the person's title. For example, if a card reads Mgr. Petra Havlova, it would be most proper to address her as *Paní magistra Havlova*, or even simply

Paní magistra. A boss may be called *Pan
director*, Mr. Director, a female doctor *Paní
doktorka*. In English, it may be easier to stick
with Mr. and Ms./Mrs. or Doctor but the best
policy is to ask. Czech President Václav Klaus,
who was an economics professor before entering
politics, is still sometimes jokingly called *Pan
professor* in the press.

Foreigners will naturally be afforded some
leeway in navigating the sea of titles and
hierarchy, but when in doubt, it's best to be as
formal and deferential as possible.

WEALTH AND MONEY

During the Communist era, especially by the 1970s,
material wealth was at least relatively equal—nearly
everyone had a job, a place to live, a holiday or two
each year within the "approved" Communist travel
zones, and basic goods. Party bigwigs had more—
cars, Western goods, more freedom to travel—and
certain marginalized groups such as those whose
politics were deemed "incorrect" had much less, but
overall society had achieved a certain equilibrium.

With the collapse of the system, both the floor
and ceiling were removed. People suddenly had
the freedom to achieve much higher levels of
wealth and material success, but the basic "rights"
included in the Communist system—a guaranteed

job and apartment, for example—were also taken away quite rapidly. For young people and those with marketable skills, vast opportunities opened, but for many middle-aged and older people, the changes were harsh and unforgiving.

Attitudes toward wealth in the Czech Republic can be explained in part by a joke commonly told about other post-Communist countries as well.

Leveling Down

An American, a Scotsman, and a Czech find a magic lamp while hiking in the woods. When they try to rub it clean, a genie emerges and offers to grant each of them a wish. The American says, "My neighbor has a beautiful mansion in the hills of Montana and plenty of cattle, and I don't. I'd like to have his house and cattle." With a wave of the genie's hand, the American is transported to his new life. The Scotsman says, "My neighbor has a beautiful flock of sheep and a cozy cottage in the heather, and I don't. I'd like to have his cottage and sheep." Magically, he finds himself in the Highlands on his new farm. The Czech says, "My neighbor has a big house on the outskirts of Prague and a farm with goats. I'd like you to set fire to the house and kill the goats."

This is not simply a matter of jealousy or a desire for goods, but of not wanting others to prosper beyond what is seen as "normal."

In the post-Communist era, accruing extensive material wealth is seen largely as the product of shady, even criminal, activities. Wealthy foreigners are often assumed to be involved in organized crime, and those Czechs who acquire wealth are often believed to be in league with organized crime or other kinds of cronyism.

It is certainly not in good taste in the Czech Republic to brag about one's material fortune, even if everyone is curious—and always ready to ask—about how much your salary is, how much you pay for rent, or how much the renovation of your weekend cottage cost (see page 72). Much more common is for a Czech to denigrate his or her situation, complaining about low salaries and high costs. In a way, there sometimes seems to be a contest of material suffering in everyday conversations, even while real wealth is growing among many sectors of the population, at least in urban areas.

Czechs in general believe that foreigners in and outside the country—at least those from the West—enjoy a much higher standard of living than they do, and that attitude has affected morality around some pricing structures. For example, taxi drivers routinely cheat foreigners or those they perceive to be foreigners because "they [foreigners] can afford it," an attitude that polls show a surprising number of Czechs support.

NOSTALGIA

Despite the wave of optimism and excitement about the downfall of Communism in 1989, waves of nostalgia for the old system have swept the Czech Republic—and much of the rest of the post-Communist region—in recent years.

One of the Czech private television stations attracted huge ratings nationwide when it rebroadcast a Communist-era television show, and recent movies highlighting the Communist 1980s have been box-office gold. Old national products such as Kofola cola drink are also enjoying a revival, even while Coke advertises on every street corner.

Do the Czechs really want a return to Communism? No, but experts say that the nostalgia trend points to a desire to in part go back to a time in which life was more certain—more limited, more frustrating, and more absurd, surely—but lacking the upheavals and insecurity of today's Czech society.

NATIONAL PRIDE

Experts say the recent nostalgia wave also reflects a desire to escape from the unrelenting influence of global and pan-European culture, which can be overwhelming to a small country. The Czechs are justifiably proud of the national culture that they have produced—from composers to playwrights to artists to authors, and beyond—and fear that their unique culture will be swept away as Czechs turn from local cuisine to worldwide ethnic food and from Czech pop stars to international superstars.

That desire to support Czech culture manifests itself in huge "all-Czech" music sections in

record stores, the dubbing of nearly all programs on Czech television into Czech regardless of the original language, and the great attention given to Czechs who gain even modest measures of international recognition. All Czechs who appear for any reason on the international stage are referred to in Czech as *naše*, "ours."

International athletic competition is one area in which national pride is obvious. In Czech TV

Olympic broadcasts, for example, it is far more common to see a Czech swimmer take fifth in a race heat over and over again than it is to see a rebroadcast of the actual medal event. When the Czechs won the gold medal in hockey—the national sport—in the 1998 Nagano Olympics, tens of thousands of people crammed themselves into Old Town Square to watch the event live on huge screens. Productivity ground to a halt throughout the tournament, and the final victory was even commemorated in a recent Czech opera, *Nagano*.

RELIGION

While opinion polls show that 80 to 90 percent of Americans consider themselves religious—a figure that sets the United States apart from many other Western nations—the Czech Republic is unique on the other end of the spectrum. Statistics indicate that as many as 68 percent of Czechs classify themselves as being "without religious belief," with a high proportion of those declaring themselves to be openly atheist or agnostic.

Of those who are religious, the largest number subscribe to Roman Catholicism (27 percent), with an additional 5 percent belonging to a Protestant denomination and 3 percent holding

Orthodox beliefs. Church attendance is low—only 12 percent of Czechs say they go to church regularly. By contrast, only 10 percent of Slovaks consider themselves to be atheists, and the Catholic Church is a powerful force there, attracting more than 60 percent of the population.

Judaism was a strong minority religion until the Second World War, but of the nearly 125,000 Jewish citizens who lived in the Czech and Moravian territories before the Nazi occupation, nearly 90,000 were deported and almost 80,000 died. After the war, approximately 10,000 Jewish survivors returned to the Czech lands, but by 1948 Communist laws forbade religious practice and many fled to avoid persecution. By the post-Communist era, it was estimated that only 6,000 Jews—most elderly—were left in the country, according to the book *Synagogues Without Jews*.

In short, Czechs today are almost peculiarly—and proudly—atheistic, and there are any number of explanations for that. Part of it stems from the associations of Roman Catholicism with the destruction of Hussitism and absorption into the Habsburg empire. Catholicism has come to be seen by some not as a religion but as a tool of national oppression. Others say it relates to the Communist past, in which religion was officially banned. Certainly the destruction of the vibrant Jewish community also plays a role.

Czech psychiatrist Libor Growsky, quoted in a *Los Angeles Times* article reprinted at About.com, explains it this way: "I'm a nonbeliever. It's connected to our history. Religion limited the freedom of the people. I don't see a difference between the Communists and the Catholics. They each want people to comply with their ideals. My sense of morality comes from literature and my family."

chapter three

FESTIVALS & CUSTOMS

As in much of the rest of the Western world, many holidays in the Czech Republic are observed only nominally, as days off from work. Traffic will be lighter, public transportation slower, and small shops and government agencies closed, but beyond that, there might be no way for a visitor to know that it's a state holiday.

That said, when Czechs do decide to celebrate—whether for a special holiday like Christmas or a notable occasion such as a name day or wedding—there are definite customs and traditions observed that may be unexpected to an outsider.

THE CHRISTMAS SEASON

The biggest holiday on the Czech calendar is Christmas, with formal holidays extending from December 24 through 26. The Christmas season kicks off much earlier, however, with December 5, Mikuláš (St. Nicholas' Eve), the unofficial start date.

On that date, the streets of the city fill with groups of costumed figures: angels, devils, and St. Nicholases. The tradition is for groups of the three to visit individual apartments to see the children of the household. All Czech children know that if they haven't been good, the devil can take them away in a sack on Mikuláš. The role of the angel is to protect the children from the devil, while St. Nicholas elicits a song or poem from the children and gives them a little present in return.

If you ask a Czech adult about Mikuláš, many will readily admit that in their childhood December 5 was one of the most stressful days on the calendar. The "best" devils are remarkably frightening-looking, especially for small children— with blackened faces, wild wigs, horns, tails, and a sack with chains—and it is ingrained from an early age that the devil and his sack are more than ready to take naughty children back to hell.

For visitors, Mikuláš is a wonderful time to be in the center of Prague. Old Town Square fills with people of all ages and countless trios of the three main players. Even little babies in carriages wear the small, electric devil horns for sale at the holiday market that springs up around this time in the square.

It's safe to say that many such notions would not play well in North America, but in the Czech Republic, it's a much-anticipated way to kick off the Christmas celebrations.

As Christmas draws closer, other traditions get underway as well. Christmas cookies in vast number and variety are considered required work in most families, and the family bakers start several weeks in advance to craft the tiny masterpieces, many of which are designed to "age" in the weeks before Christmas. From crumbly almond crescents to intricately molded marzipan beehives, the cookies on offer in Czech households will delight and astound. Unfortunately for visitors, very few of the baked goods and only the most common varieties are sold in commercial stores—the handcrafting necessary doesn't lend itself to mass marketing.

About a week before Christmas, live Christmas tree stands and—more confusingly for visitors— huge aluminum tanks appear in the public squares and on busy street corners. The tanks are filled with live carp, the official Christmas dish of the Czech Republic. Carp buyers can choose to take their fish home live, where they will be kept in the bathtub until Christmas Eve, or they can have them "whacked" and processed there on the street.

The fish entrails are never thrown away, as they create the basis for the soup that is the first course of the Christmas dinner. The carp itself is fried in batter, and served traditionally with potato salad. Non-fish-eaters might be offered *kuřeci řízek* (breaded chicken breast prepared like Wiener schnitzel). Sometimes a special rolled sausage will be served as well.

Carp may not seem like the most obvious Christmas dish, but the popular theory is that carp was a cheap enough "centerpiece" to be affordable for everyone, even peasants. Carp is also a traditional Christmas dish in parts of Poland and Germany.

Czech families celebrate the gift-giving portion of the holidays on December 24, and that is also the traditional day for the big Christmas dinner. The Christmas tree is a part of the celebration, but it is put up on Christmas Eve, once the children have been taken somewhere else. Once the tree is decorated and the presents are in place, a small bell is rung to signify that Ježíšek—the Czech equivalent of Santa Claus whose name literally means "Little Jesus" but is not a religious figure—has come and the children can return. The number of presents is more important than the size or scale of the items, and the opening can take many hours.

Christmas is very much considered to be a private family holiday, so it is somewhat unlikely that a visitor new to the country would be invited to take part in the celebration. Still, visitors can involve themselves in the season by wandering through the markets, eating at a restaurant that offers Christmas carp (*kapr*), or attending a church service.

Christmas Eve, Christmas Day, and the day after Christmas (St. Stephen's Day) are considered state holidays, and many businesses and all government agencies will be closed. Because of the three-day holidays for Christmas and the status of January 1, New Year's Day, as a state holiday as well, some companies simply don't bother to open between Christmas and New Year. Even those businesses that do stay open are likely to be manned by skeleton crews, since the holiday season is a favorite time for package vacations as well.

Given the closures and low staffing levels, the holiday season is a singularly bad choice for a business trip and can even be problematic for a pleasure visit, at least on the state holidays. Dining and shopping choices even in central Prague will be limited, and outside the capital— with the possible exception of ski resorts—it can seem like visiting a ghost town.

NEW YEAR'S EVE AND NEW YEAR'S DAY

New Year's Eve is called "Silvestr" in Czech and is celebrated with lavish parties, dinners, and fireworks—largely by non-Czechs. The traditional Praguer way to spend Silvestr is to leave the city for a small private party at a *chata*, or ski cottage. Most visitors will find themselves in one of the central squares or at the castle to watch the fireworks, which are indeed spectacular but can also be dangerous. Fireworks are sold in myriad retail outlets for several weeks leading up to the holiday, and there are no restrictions on who can buy them. Basic safety rules about lighting (and throwing!) fireworks in crowds are not observed.

As such, Prague tourist centers including Old Town Square, Wenceslas Square, and the castle district are not good spots for families with children on New Year's Eve. The danger factor is simply too high. For the adventurous, however, the celebration is huge and infectious, if sometimes quite cold.

Restaurants traditionally offer a "Silvestr-Menu," a multicourse meal and champagne, instead of their usual fare, and it's important to check the price before sitting down. Such menus are almost always more expensive than regular offerings, sometimes ridiculously so. Be aware.

New Year's Day is the actual state holiday, and in addition to marking the start of the new year it commemorates Independent Czech State Renewal Day, the date in 1993 when Czechoslovakia split into the Czech Republic and Slovakia. It is not traditionally celebrated with anything more involved than a day off from work to nurse Silvestr hangovers.

EASTER

Given the Czechs' overall lack of affection for organized religion, it is perhaps not surprising that they have put their own spin on Easter traditions. While the faithful do observe the Lenten and Easter season in ways that would be familiar to Christians around the world, on Easter Monday—also the state holiday of the period— the Czechs have their own pagan-origin way to celebrate.

For a week or so before Easter, braided willow switches ranging from tiny to giant are on sale in flower shops and markets. On Easter Monday, men wield the switches to whip women around the ankles. The women—who by tradition are supposed to want to be whipped by as many men as possible—respond to the whipping not by slugging the men but by presenting them with eggs. Men are supposed to want to collect as many eggs as possible.

Although the tradition has been questioned by some outsiders and feminists, most Czechs see it as harmless fun. However, some women admit to dreading the day because of overeager male relatives, and the practice is less popular than it once was in urban areas.

SPRING WEDDINGS, SUMMER HOLIDAYS

As the sun returns in the spring, the wedding season ramps up at local town halls. As in most European countries, Czechs must have a civil ceremony to make their nuptials official, and Prague's spectacular Old Town Hall on the Old Town Square is a favorite spot. In April and June (May weddings are considered unlucky), the Old Town Hall turns into a virtual assembly line of civil ceremonies, with bridal couples in and out every ten minutes. Once joined, the wedding parties head to waiting cars decorated with flowery window ribbons and small bride and groom figures to go to the reception. The motorcade will then honk its way through town, and it is entirely proper—if not impossible to resist—to wave and smile as they pass.

Both May 1 and 8 are state holidays, honoring May Day for workers and the end of the Second World War, respectively. Parades and demonstrations are not uncommon on May Day, especially among anti-globalization forces, far-right groups, and Communists, and sometimes violence has erupted when the disparate groups meet. However, since the riots of 2000 during a world meeting of the International Monetary Fund, the Czech police have become more adept with crowd control, and as such, the demonstrations in recent years have stayed calm. Many Czechs also mark May 5, which was the beginning of the Czech uprising against Germany at the end of the Second World War in 1945, but it's not a formal holiday.

The *Maturita*

Another spring rite of passage is the *Maturita*, a state exam given in May and June to secondary school students to allow them to graduate and go on to university (if they can then pass the university entrance exams). The two-part test dates from the mid-nineteenth century, and students must conquer both the written and oral exams in several subjects to pass. Approximately 40 percent of all Czechs have passed the test, and to do so is

still considered cause for celebration and honor. In the weeks leading up to the tests, small groups of potential graduates will gather in high-traffic areas such as public transportation stops and squares to raise money for the parties that are held on completion of the exams. Putting a few coins in the can is sure to be appreciated—and the money is likely to be spent on drink.

Summer Vacations

As in most other European countries, summer vacations are taken seriously in the Czech Republic. For their part, Czechs flee the cities for the fresh air of their *chatas* in the summer, and weekends almost universally start early on Friday afternoons. Weekends are spent in the country, and most Czechs will also spend two weeks or more on vacation abroad. The Czech Republic, like most other European countries, offers generous paid vacation to its citizens. Employers are required to give their employees four weeks of paid vacation leave, and many employers tack an additional week onto that. Czech law also states that one vacation should be at least two weeks in length, so many workers take advantage of that stipulation to go on one of the many popular and affordable package vacations to sunny destinations. At least 10 percent will go to the seaside of Croatia.

Given the high probability that vast swathes of working Czechs will be taking a "Czech Friday" or be on vacation during the summer months (roughly mid-June to September 1), showing up to conduct business is not advised during this time. Delays can stretch to weeks as waves of employees leave for vacation.

The holidays that fall on July 5 and 6—commemorating the arrival of Christianity in the Slavic lands in the ninth century, and the burning of the religious and linguistic reformer Jan Hus at the stake in 1415—take a particular toll on productivity as the two-day holiday often stretches longer. Such vacation largesse may well be too depressing for vacation-starved Americans to cope with on a business trip. Best to wait until the fall.

FALL CELEBRATIONS

Fall sees three state holidays, all commemorating Czech nationhood in some form. On September 28, Czech Statehood Day honors the Czech patron saint, Václav (Wenceslas). A month later, in October, the state recognizes Independent Czechoslovak State Proclamation Day, which marks the founding of the state of Czechoslovakia in 1918. After the Velvet Revolution, November 17 was declared the "Day of the Fight for Freedom and Democracy" in honor of demonstrators—many of whom were students—who rose up against the the Nazis in 1939 and the Communists in 1989. The day is marked mostly by the presence of small shrines with burning candles at significant spots throughout Prague.

Many Czechs also observe a sort of Memorial Day on November 2, once the Day of the Dead (All Souls' Day) in the Church calendar. It is not a holiday from work and no longer has religious connotations, but people visit and tend the graves of loved ones on this day. Czech cemeteries tend to be beautifully kept up throughout the year.

Fall is also mushroom-picking season for legions of Czechs. Wild mushrooms (*houby*) are used year-round by drying and pickling the fall's harvest, and most every family has a special mushroom spot. A few Czechs every year die from eating poisonous mushrooms, but given how many do it, it's a testament to Czech horticultural knowledge that the number is as low as it is.

BIRTHDAYS AND NAME DAYS

For Czechs, "name days" (*svátky*) are actually more important than birthdays. Each day of the calendar corresponds to the name of a saint, and on that day, anyone who shares the name of that saint will celebrate his or her name day. It is customary to offer a toast and a small gift such as flowers or chocolates or a greeting card. (It is vital to remember that only an odd number of flowers should be given as a gift. Even numbers signify funereal arrangements!)

In an office setting, it is not unusual for coworkers to gather to celebrate a name day with champagne and an exchange of good wishes. Name days for the week are often posted outside flower shops and also appear in most newspapers, including the English-language *Prague Post*.

Birthdays are also celebrated, but on a smaller scale than name days. In addition, the person celebrating the birthday is customarily expected to provide the refreshments, which may seem strange to North Americans. If you are invited to a restaurant for a Czech person's birthday, for example, it would be tradition that the person having the birthday would pay for the dinner, although it would be appreciated if the guests were to bring flowers or another small gift. At the office, a person having a birthday may bring in his or her own cake and champagne to share with the rest of the staff.

HOLIDAYS AND THE CZECH YEAR

January 1 Independent Czech State Renewal Day, New Year

March/April Easter Monday

May 1 Labor Day

May 8 Liberation Day

July 5 Cyril and Methodius Day

July 6 Jan Hus Day

September 28 Czech Statehood Day

October 28 Independent Czechoslovak State Proclamation Day

November 17 Day of Fight for Freedom and Democracy

December 24 Christmas Eve

December 25 Christmas Day

December 26 St. Stephen's Day

chapter four

MAKING FRIENDS

The best way to appreciate a culture is to get to know the people who make it up. However, for visitors to the Czech Republic who may have only a few days in the country, the possibility of making friends with Czechs may be remote. Of course it will be Czechs staffing shops and museums, restaurants and pubs, but most people in the service industry—as in North America—are not looking to socialize with their clientele.

Those visitors who have the privilege of staying a little longer—or interacting in a workplace situation—may find it easier. If getting to know ordinary Czechs is a goal of your visit, you will have to work a little harder than the average tourist, but the effort will be worth it for the lifetime friendships you may be able to have.

FORMALITY RULES THE DAY

It's important to understand how Czechs conduct their own social lives. Most Americans will find the level of formality in standard social settings confusing and even intimidating, but it's vital to maintain that respectful distance or risk offense.

As in many other languages, Czech has a formal and informal "you" for addressing others—*ty* for children, animals, and close friends or family and *vy* for pretty much everyone else. (Such a distinction was once made in English using "you" and "thou," but that level of formality dropped out of the language.) It is unlikely as a visitor that Czech will be your lingua franca, but an understanding of this distinction is important— perhaps more culturally than linguistically.

Here's an example: two elderly ladies have lived across the hall from each other in an apartment building for more than fifty years. They have watched as governments have fallen, children have grown up, and spouses have passed away. They see each other every day in the hall and at the mailboxes. How do they greet each other? Using the formal *vy* and their last names (for example, *Paní* [Mrs.] Novakova). Even though a level of intimacy exists between them, they do not consider themselves to be friends, just acquaintances. As such, the two ladies cannot switch to the informal *ty* without causing confusion and possibly offense.

The same is true in the workplace. Most colleagues who have worked together for years will always refer to each other using *vy* and last names. Younger workers or those who see each other socially outside of work may use the informal *ty*, but it would be highly unusual for that informality to extend beyond a select few. (Further issues of hierarchy, names, and formality in the workplace will be addressed in Chapter 8.)

Among young people—especially university-age students—the rules relax. Few young Czechs would go clubbing with acquaintances and call them Mr. Janáček and Mrs. Vrbová on the dance floor, of course.

Still, the safest course for visitors is to assume formality. Although you will be unlikely to use Czech *vy* and *ty* in addressing people, you should use a last name with anyone to whom you are introduced, especially in an office setting—within the bounds of common sense. If someone introduces themselves to you simply as Jana, for example, you should feel free to use first names in talking. But the Czech should make the call.

While on the subject of "Jana," it merits mention that many Czechs will assume that their actual Czech name is too difficult for an English speaker to decipher and so will Anglicize it. This could lead to a foreigner being introduced to a room of full of Janes, Georges, and Peters. It can be confusing, and it is acceptable for a visitor to ask for the Czech versions—but be ready to try to pronounce them properly!

MAKING CONVERSATION

Meeting ordinary Czechs who are out socializing—in a bar, restaurant, or club setting, for example—can be challenging, even given the phenomenon of the shared table in many establishments. It is not the custom to start conversations with strangers in the Czech Republic, although there are things you can do to make such chance encounters more probable.

As in most places, making contact with strangers will be easier if you are alone or with only a small group. (Naturally, using common sense about this, particularly if you are a single woman traveling alone, is imperative.) Few things are more intimidating than a large group of people speaking a foreign language—especially at the decibel level common among North Americans—so if you're looking to meet Czechs, keep the group small and the conversation to a dull roar.

Learning a few phrases in Czech will also be helpful. Czechs are very proud of their language and are happy and pleased when foreigners try to speak with them in Czech. Asking a Czech for help with the language is generally a good way to start a conversation. Asking for directions or recommendations can also be an inroad.

If you do find yourself engaged in conversation with a Czech or group of Czechs, you can expect the discussion to be wide-ranging and deep. Czechs tend to be well-educated and highly literate and are generally not afraid to voice opinions about politics or religion that might be too controversial to bring up in your home country. Voicing your own opinions is expected and welcomed, but be prepared to be questioned closely about ideas you might express.

Of course, small talk is more common at first, and there are topics that are likely to come up again and again when foreigners and Czechs meet (see also pages 143 and 153).

Most Czechs will want to know what you think of the Czech Republic and Czechs, and especially how you would compare things to conditions and people in your home country. It is not unusual to be asked directly, "Why did you come to the Czech Republic and what do you think of Prague/the Czech people/the country?" You may want to think about your answers before you find yourself trying to come up with things on the fly.

The most dangerous question of those you are likely to be asked is, "What do you dislike about the Czech Republic and the Czechs?" Perhaps strange to visitors, this is a common question that all Czechs seem to want an answer to. The big balancing act with this question is that most Czechs don't actually want it answered *honestly*. Just as in discussing one's own family it is permitted to criticize a family member personally but someone outside the family's engaging in such talk is likely to be met with hurt feelings or even anger, Czechs don't mind hearing a few minor dislikes but are apt to disengage from conversation with someone who speaks harshly about their country.

This is not to say that you should lie and say that you like everything about the Czech Republic and its people if that's not what you feel, just that it is imperative to be judicious about the things you choose to tell Czech people. If you are in full culture shock mode after a particularly unpleasant encounter with a shop attendant, rant to a friend in an e-mail, not to the nice Czech person you met at a restaurant who has already taken a chance by talking with you.

Here is an example of one possible category of answer to the dreaded question: "I am so happy to be able to spend time in this beautiful country. Prague is beautiful and there is so much history! I've liked everything I've seen here. If I had to come up with a complaint, I guess it would be that it's sometimes hard to get around because the street signs are difficult to locate and I feel intimidated when approaching people I don't know to ask directions because Czech is such a difficult language."

Such an answer will speak to a desire on your part to get to know the city better—and may even result in an offer for a local's tour, which is by far the best kind. Moreover, it gets in a statement about the difficulty of the language, which is both flattering to Czechs and a kind of small apology for your own lack of skill in Czech.

Questions about financial situations and specifics is an unexpected (for North Americans, especially) but common thread as well. One of the worst remarks that can be made is how cheap everything is in the Czech Republic. While it is true that you will find some things less expensive in the Czech Republic—although that is less and less true as the crown gains strength—for locals, things have become incredibly expensive in a short amount of time, especially in Prague. Still, it's very likely that you may be asked how prices and wages compare to your home country, and it's best to adopt a neutral attitude of some things being a better value and some things being more expensive. It's entirely honest and spares you from looking like a rich tourist who doesn't understand the situation on the ground for locals.

It's also fair for you to refuse to answer

specific questions that you may be asked but don't want to answer about how much you earn, how much you are paying for your accommodation, how much the tourist trinket you just bought cost you, etc. Czechs love to tell visitors when they have been ripped off, but such conversations are no fun for the person who has been taken, especially because there is almost no recourse.

FRIENDSHIP

Most Czechs make their friends the same way people everywhere do—in their hometowns, schools, and universities, and through common interests. In general, making a friend in the workplace takes a little longer because of the formality that persists at work, but some Czechs do socialize with colleagues as well.

It is not uncommon for Czechs to maintain friendships through many years and circumstances, and many have friends from high school or even before who are still considered dear to them. Because Czechs on the whole are less mobile than people in the United States— tending to stay in their place of birth for schooling and beyond much more frequently than Americans, for example—longstanding friendships are easier to maintain.

Groups of friends often socialize together, traveling on weekends to someone's *chata* or going to restaurants. Once accepted by a Czech or into a group of Czechs as a friend, a foreigner is likely to find warmth and wit—but breaking into that circle is far from easy, given the length and background of most Czech relationships.

CZECH HOSPITALITY

It may take some time and concerted effort to meet Czechs, but when you do get to know someone well enough to be the recipient of hospitality, it will all seem worth it. With friends and acquaintances, Czechs are incredibly generous and bighearted. Such intimacy does not come about instantly, but it can last a lifetime.

A Night at the *Hospoda*

The most common social invitation from a Czech would be for a beer or two at a *hospoda* (pub). The person doing the inviting would expect to pay, although it is polite to offer to buy subsequent rounds, depending on whether the pub asks for payment per round or at the end.

On the subject of alcohol and beer in particular—Czechs are especially proud of the quality of their beer (*pivo*), as well they should be—there is a Czech saying that on evenings out, you only have two beers: the first and the last. Expect to be cajoled to drink not just one beer but many, and if you're a teetotaler, a pub may not be your best bet. Ask if there is a local coffee shop or teahouse where you might be able to have a quieter conversation.

Also, many more Czechs smoke than do North Americans, and pubs are free-for-all smoking zones. If you are extremely sensitive to cigarette smoke, mention it in advance, but don't expect to be accommodated. There is a feeling that North Americans are unnecessarily puritanical when it comes to secondhand smoke, and while individuals with whom you are socializing may agree not to smoke at the table with you, other pub patrons will not.

Going Out for a Meal

The next level of hospitality you might experience would be an invitation to a restaurant. Again, the person issuing the invitation would expect to pay, although offers of contributions would not be insulting but are likely to be rebuffed. Strong food preferences should be expressed in advance—especially vegetarianism, because not all restaurants have vegetarian options—but again, you may get some gentle ribbing about such "North Americanism."

If you are taken to a Czech restaurant, expect to be asked how you like Czech food, and, if you're game, ask for recommendations about local specialties. Most Czechs love to explain their culinary traditions and will also be happy to decipher menu options that might seems impenetrable, even in English—Spanish bird and Moravian sparrow, anyone? (For more information about Czech food, see Chapter 6.)

Invitations Home

Invitations to visit a Czech at his or her home should be taken seriously as a sign of true friendship. Such invitations are not given lightly, and there are some general things to expect when visiting a Czech home.

If you are given a specific time to arrive, try to be punctual. Chances are good that your host will be preparing multiple dishes that may have tricky timing. Upon arrival, be sure to offer to take off your shoes. Czechs always remove their shoes indoors and usually have slippers that they wear while inside. You may be offered slippers or told that you can leave your shoes on. Unless you are very uncomfortable in bare or stocking feet, take off your shoes. It's the polite thing to do.

It is generally expected that a guest will be offered a meal. Sunday lunch is a common "big" meal in Czech households, and the cuisine on

offer is likely to be traditional Czech food.
Expect multiple courses of both food and drink,
and bring your appetite! A typical Sunday lunch
might include an aperitif, salad, soup, entrée, and
side dish with wine or beer, and dessert with
coffee or tea. Bohemian *Sekt* (sparkling wine) is
often offered as an apéritif or with dessert, and
Becherovka (a spicy herbal liqueur) is very often
served after the meal. Toasts are common but
not elaborate.

It is not recommended that guests bring any
food to share at the meal, as that can be seen as
an insult to the host. The notion of potluck
dinners is not common. That doesn't mean guests
should come empty-handed, however. It is
considered good manners to bring flowers (again,
not an even number), a bottle of wine, and
possibly a box of chocolates. A bottle of whiskey
or another imported hard liquor would be an
appropriate gift for a man.

A handwritten note sent
through the mail is a nice
touch after you have
been the recipient of
hospitality in a Czech
home. Photos of the
occasion, if any were taken,
are also greatly prized and
should be included with the note.

Reciprocation is not expected but is always appreciated. As a visitor, your options are probably more limited, but inviting someone out to a restaurant after he or she has hosted you at home would be entirely appropriate.

CZECH NAMES

It may seem to a North American visitor that there are only a handful of names in use in the Czech Republic because certain common ones tend to crop up again and again. It is true that compared to English (especially American English), Czech has fewer names considered to be "acceptable." And parents must submit the names they are planning to give their children to a sort of "name police"—a government bureaucrat—to determine that the name is suitable to give a child. This means that there are certainly fewer Moon Units and Rainbows in the Czech Republic, but a lot more Petras, Jans, Zdeněks, and Pavlas. And Czechs do not use middle names, so finding the proper Radek Dolezal in the phonebook can be a real challenge.

As an aside, it may be helpful to know that women's last names almost always end with –ová in Czech, a construct that the language deems grammatically necessary to talk about women. What this means for visitors is that you might find your own name "Czechified"—for example, if you are Susan Johnson, you will likely be called Mrs. Johnsonová in a formal setting. Even foreign celebrities are given the *–ová* treatment when they are discussed in Czech—Julia Robertsová, Hillary Clintonová, and Margaret Thatcherová, to name a few.

AT HOME

HOUSING

Most short-term visitors to the Czech Republic
will not get the chance to see an ordinary Czech
home up close. All who visit Prague and fly into
the airport will see *where* many Czechs live—in
paneláky (huge Communist-era apartment blocks
made of concrete panels)—but the average visitor
is unlikely to get up close and personal.

Although times are
changing and home
ownership is on the
rise, the majority of
Czechs still live in
apartment buildings—
many of them on the

outskirts of cities. In Prague alone, as many as
80,000 people live in the densely inhabited
suburbs of Prague 4 (called *jižní město*—south
town), which is served by the metro's C line.

Quality, affordable housing in cities remains a
problem, largely because the aging *paneláky* do
not lend themselves to either update and

renovation or even just plain destruction. Built from the outside to stand the test of time—the concrete panels that form the structure of the buildings are reputed to be impervious even to dynamite blasts—their dilapidated interiors are crumbling to the point of making some barely habitable. The Prague municipal government is trying to reclaim and renovate the capital's *paneláky*, but it is slow work, especially as wealthier people leave the structures—and indeed the urban center—to build houses in Prague's outskirts.

The ownership structure and history of pre-Communist apartment blocks in the Czech Republic also makes renovation difficult. In the Communist era, residential buildings were nationalized and taken from original owners and then units were assigned to citizens by the government. Rent paid was nominal, but there was also no chance of claiming a primary living space as one's own.

When the Communist government fell in 1989, the government began the slow process of reprivatizing nationalized buildings, and returning them to the owners or the heirs of owners who had had property appropriated after 1948, a process called restitution. While those who were able to reclaim restituted property suddenly found themselves in possession of what was in some cases extremely valuable real estate, the possibilities for doing anything with the buildings were limited by long-standing tenants and the protections afforded them.

Those tenants—some of whom had lived in the same apartments for decades and were by now quite elderly—could not simply be kicked out onto the curb, so a compensation process was put in place. In general, a building owner has to "buy out" these tenants—usually a substantial cash payment, in addition to procuring new lodgings for them—in order to reclaim their space, and cannot unduly raise their rents due to strict rent control. The laws have made for some interesting conflicts in Prague's hot real estate scene, including the famous story of the elderly man living in a spacious old flat on the street leading to the Charles Bridge and paying less than $50 a month to do so.

Property owners and those who had property returned to them have banded together to try to get more rights, but the process has been slow. And for every landlord who cries foul over not being able to charge market value for his or her apartments, or to renovate crumbling apartments to make them more attractive, there is an elderly person who can tell tales of being threatened by an aggressive property owner to leave or else. It's a situation with no winners at the present, and one

that will take at least a
generation to right itself.

Those buildings that did not
have single owners before the
Communist takeover have met
various fates. Some have
been privatized into co-op
arrangements, in which longtime apartment
dwellers could buy their homes or pass them
along to family members for very reasonable
prices. Some have been sold to local or
international investors for wholesale renovation
and reentry into the market at prevailing rates.
Still others have been razed to the ground to make
way for new housing that can be rented or sold.

Mortgages for houses and apartments are
increasingly common, and the Czech government
has even set up incentive savings programs for
young Czechs to enable them to buy a house or
apartment. Property ownership is seen very much
as something to strive for in the Czech Republic,
especially among the educated urban middle
class, although Prague's hot real estate market is
pricing many out of the possibility.

THE CZECH FAMILY

Czech families tend to be close-knit, with family
members living near one another for most of their

lives. It is common for children to go to a university located close enough to allow them to live at home, and even Czechs who emigrate today often do so with the hope of earning enough money to allow them to come back to the Czech Republic to live.

Extended family relations are very important, with grandparents playing a significant role. Many times, grandmothers will serve as primary caregivers of their grandchildren, allowing their own children to go out to work.

Czechs tend to have small families who often live together until children are grown and married, although that is changing as society becomes more affluent. During the Communist era,  it was not uncommon for extended families to have to live together due to the shortage of available housing. Communal housing as was seen in the Soviet Union was never common, but relatively large numbers of related people being forced to live together in small spaces was the standard situation.

Children stayed in their parents' houses until—and sometimes beyond—marriage. Since one of the few ways to get an apartment of one's own in the Communist era was to marry and have children, Czechs in this time period tended to get married and have children quite young. Divorce was—and remains—common, although it is no longer the case that many divorced people are forced to continue to live together after divorcing because of the Communist-era housing shortage.

As the housing problem has abated, marriage ages have gone up and the marriage rate overall has dropped to historic lows. In addition, Czechs have one of the lowest fertility rates in the world, leading some Czech nationalists to question the long-term survival prospects of the Czechs as a nation. Few experts are willing to go that far, but there certainly seems to be a reluctance on the part of Czechs to have children, despite relatively generous (by North American standards, anyway) pro-natal governmental policies including three-plus years of maternity/paternity leave with guaranteed return employment, a one-time birth payment that increases for subsequent children, and a small monthly stipend to support stay-at-home parents.

The inverted population structure that is expected in the Czech Republic as the population ages—as in much of the rest of the industrialized world—will certainly hit the Czech social system hard, and the country is likely to face hard choices about immigration and social services.

THE *CHATA*

One thing that has not changed since 1989 is the Czechs' abiding affection for the *chata* or *chalupy*—the weekend cottage—that ranges in sophistication from tiny lean-to shacks to year-round inhabitable second homes. The importance of going to the *chata* has influenced everything from the Czech love of and skill in gardening and DIY work to the way workweeks are scheduled.

In the Communist era, weekend cottages represented the only chance for Czechs to own a small plot of land, and they used this ability to craft largely homemade structures where the extended family could get together on weekends and for weeks at a time during the summer. Getting back to nature is perceived as very important to Czechs, especially those who live in big cities, in part because of the belief that fresh, country air is vital for health—not far-fetched, given the air quality in Prague and other Czech urban and industrial centers. While industrial and brown coal air pollution have markedly decreased since 1989, air pollution from automobiles has risen dramatically. Many residents view their summer and weekend *chata* time as a chance for their lungs to refresh themselves after the long, often gray-aired Prague winters.

Starting around the May holidays, Czechs fix up their makeshift trailers and begin to haul equipment and supplies to their weekend cottages. By the time school ends in June, the *chata* is set for the season, and families begin to extend their weekends to weeks. During *chata* season, it is not unusual for people to leave work by early Friday afternoon to try to avoid the rush of cars headed out of the city. (And lines of cars start to make the exodus by 3:00 p.m. or even earlier, so if you ever want to drive out of Prague in the spring and summer, choose some time other than Friday afternoon!) During the weekends, Prague's residential areas can seem like ghost towns, with parking places galore and streets so quiet as to seem completely uninhabited.

Activities at the *chata* unsurprisingly revolve around family, with gardening, hiking, and biking, and home improvement topping the list of things to do. Any visitor invited to a *chata* for the weekend should try to find out if they can expect a "second home" or a "shack" experience. Both can be equally enjoyable, but one might require more preparation on the part of the visitor. Ask if you will need to bring a sleeping bag or mat and if there is running water to help figure out what is in store. No strangers to roughing it, Czechs do usually realize that visitors may expect something fancier than what is on offer, so many will try to downsize expectations even without being asked. Whatever kind of cottage is there, expect good company, garden-fresh produce, and clean air (possibly for the first time in weeks) when you head to the *chata*.

FOR THE LOVE OF CARS

Pollution from cars has made the air in Prague roughly as bad today as it was during the unrestricted industrial heyday of Communism. That fact alone well illustrates the Czech love of cars. During the Communist period, cars were a rare luxury, with waiting lists sometimes years long. When the auto market became more affordable and open to average Czechs, Czechs started to purchase their national car brand, Škoda, in droves. A huge number of those old Škodas are still on the road today, but now they have been joined by increasing numbers of new Škodas, as well as Volkswagons, Audis, and

Peugeots. It is now said that the density of car ownership in Prague is second only to Munich in Europe, and that statistic is borne out if you ever try to drive during rush hour, on Friday afternoons, or Sunday evenings. In truth, traffic is increasingly bad all the time, especially given that roads in Prague were hardly set up to accommodate the ever-increasing number of vehicles.

Just like Americans, Czechs love to drive their cars to work, the grocery store, and the mall, and carpooling is nearly unheard of. A nascent environmental, anti-car movement has organized a few demonstrations and protests, but it seems unlikely that after years of being denied access to cars, the Czechs are going to give theirs up anytime soon.

EVERYDAY SHOPPING

Although there is an increasing tendency for Czech consumers to take their cars to *hypermarkets* (huge supermarkets that are sometimes also department stores) outside the center for large grocery runs, many Czechs— especially older folks—still follow the more traditional daily shopping patterns at smaller, neighborhood shops, bakeries, and fruit and vegetable stores. Neighborhood general grocery stores also remain popular, although it is hard to see how they will stay in business as the *hypermarket* concept grows in popularity.

Unlike in many European cities, there is no single, central fruit and vegetable market for produce and other fresh goods. Such markets are scattered around the city and are often mixed with stands that offer tourist junk. Fruit and vegetable stores (usually called just *Ovoce-Zelenina*) are much more popular among  locals than the open-air markets, although some passage markets, located in the entryways and spaces between buildings and often run by Vietnamese immigrants, are also popular.

Vietnamese and other Asian immigrants also run the vast majority of Prague's open-air clothing and general merchandise markets. Czechs openly deride the quality of goods purchased at such markets, but they are nearly always packed with shoppers. It is difficult to find affordable clothing in retail stores in the Czech Republic—Americans in particular will find the clothing on offer to be of lower quality and much higher price than what they are used to—which probably explains the enduring popularity of the Vietnamese markets.

Secondhand shops are also very common and can have good, quality merchandise at affordable prices.

Malls and other retail gathering spots are growing in popularity also as incomes rise. Leisure shopping is covered in Chapter 6, but some Czechs do head to the mall for everyday shopping as well, particularly as an increasing number of international retailers such as Swedish clothing giant H&M move in (see page 102).

WORK LIFE

In the Communist era, employment was guaranteed but fell under the familiar Communist saying of "I pretend to work and they pretend to pay me." That legacy lingers in some service and bureaucratic sectors (most notably the post office and other governmental utility monopolies), but is improving slowly.

Still, employees enjoy protections—and restrictions—that would shock an American. Any employer who wants to downsize his workforce must provide at least three months notice and pay to those who will be let go, and an employee wishing to leave must give between one and three month's notice. Workers are guaranteed paid vacation (four weeks by law, and many are offered additional time) and more or less unlimited sick leave, with a doctor's note.

The use of sick leave is one of those benefits that set the Czechs apart from most other industrialized countries, especially the United States. The average Czech will take twenty-nine days of sick leave *every year*, on top of the four weeks of paid holiday that is standard and the numerous state holidays. Czechs take illness seriously and will not appreciate a sick colleague coming to work—and may even be openly hostile to a sneezing, wheezing coworker. When a Czech visits the doctor for an illness or injury, it is not at all uncommon for the doctor to tell the patient that he or she will be sick for an extended period of time and unable to work.

Typical E-mails About Sick Leave

"I have flu. The doctor says I will be sick until next Friday."

"I am feeling poorly today. Tomorrow I will see doctor and he will tell me when I can come back to work."

"I am on antibiotics for ten days and cannot come to work."

"I cannot be assigned to the May project because I will be sick then."

There is a firm belief in the healing power of rest, to the exclusion—at least in the eyes of some outsiders and, indeed, businesspeople—of logic. For a course of antibiotics, a Czech employee can expect to be excused from work for the entire time he or she is taking the drug, for example. Sometimes a doctor will even ask how long a person *wants* to be out of work.

Such scenarios can be frustrating for someone visiting on business, as illness with a doctor's excuse is ironclad, even for weeks at a time. If you are visiting for only a few days and need to meet with someone specific, don't expect any sick Czech to come to work just to see you. Sick is sick, and sick and work don't mix.

THE CZECH EDUCATION SYSTEM

Czechs are justifiably proud of their educational system, which is designed to provide free, high-quality education to all students. In practice, it

has its problems—mainly surrounding the issue of funding—but the end result is that most Czechs leave school with a good basic education. The illiteracy rate in the country as a whole is under 2 percent, with ethnic

Czech illiteracy standing at less than 1 percent.

Education begins at age six with "basic school," which lasts for five years. The next phase, secondary school, (four years) is entered without selective testing, but academic selection does enter into the next level of secondary school, with students being tracked into either further academic study to prepare for university or into vocational training.

Public university is free for any student who can pass the exams of the faculty they want to attend, but across the country there are far more students who would like to attend public university—and indeed are probably fully qualified to do so—than there are places available. The result in the post-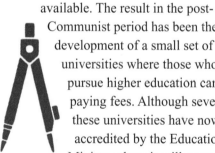Communist period has been the development of a small set of private universities where those who want to pursue higher education can do so by paying fees. Although several of these universities have now been accredited by the Education Ministry, there is still something of a stigma attached to a degree from a "private" university—public universities are still held to be far more prestigious.

The main reason that public universities cannot serve as many students as there is demand is, of course, a lack of money. Because public education is supposed to be free, attempts to charge even low levels of tuition have been met with tremendous resistance. The system cannot run without money—and taxes cannot meet all the demands of the system—and so many facilities are crumbling and professors are grumbling about their low salaries. Salaries are even lower at the primary and secondary levels, with teachers complaining that they cannot even pay basic living expenses on teacher salaries. Many teachers take on private students or second jobs to try to make ends meet.

In addition to oversubscription at the university level and general funding woes, the Czech education system has been plagued with complaints about how it treats minority students, especially those who are Roma (Gypsy). The plight of Roma in the Czech Republic in many ways stems from the failure to integrate Romani children into the education system—whether by simple neglect or by such reprehensible policies as routinely segregating them in "special schools." While Romani children have the legal right to attend state schools, many fail the entrance examinations because they don't speak Czech well enough.

This has led to further social segregation as the children grow into adults with far fewer vocational and education possibilities. The blame cannot all be placed on the state, however, given that some Romani families would prefer not to send their children to school. Regardless of who should win the blame game, the Romani issue in education and other spheres of Czech life is a thorny one, unlikely to simply fade away, especially given the European Union emphasis on minority rights.

MILITARY AND CIVIL SERVICE

For 140 years, Czechs had a tradition of compulsory military service for all young men. In 2005, that all ended with the professionalization of the armed forces and the end of conscription—a change forced in part by Czech membership in NATO. Until 2005, all Czech men had to complete a year of military service or eighteen months of civil service if they could prove that they were not "fit" for military service—which vast numbers found a way to prove through their connections with medical professionals. Civil service could mean working in a school, hospital, or nonprofit organization, for which the conscripts received salaries that totaled only half of the country's minimum wage.

Most young Czech men heaved a sigh of relief at the knowledge that they would no longer have to "do their time"—compulsory service was viewed by most who were forced to do it with chagrin and resentment because of the small salaries and basic, often messy work involved— but the change will also present a hardship for the organizations who used civil service labor to stay afloat. It's too early to determine how the transformation will affect larger society, but it is safe to say that the demise of compulsory service will not be long mourned.

chapter six

TIME OUT

As with the citizens of most other European countries, Czechs have managed to strike a fairly civilized balance between work and home. Work expectations for white-collar professions rarely stretch beyond forty hours per week—although that is changing somewhat as younger workers commit themselves more strongly to career advancement—and weekend or evening work is relatively uncommon.

Czechs value their free time, and many spend their hours of leisure in pursuits that are familiar around the world— watching television, going to movies and concerts, shopping, and participating in athletic and nature activities. It is this last category about which Czechs are particularly passionate. Whether skiing in the Krkonoše in the winter, biking on the Greenways trails in the spring, swimming at Podoli pool in the summer, or picking mushrooms in the fall, Czechs can reliably be found enjoying their natural surroundings while getting some exercise.

Therefore visitors wanting to experience "real" Czech life would be well-advised to leave some of their free time for a nature walk, even if it's only in one of Prague's public parks. But be forewarned: Czechs tend to be in excellent shape, especially where walking is concerned. If you sign up for a Czech-led hiking or walking excursion, expect to walk quickly and energetically. Some North Americans will have trouble keeping up or making it to the end.

The Czech fondness for physical activity— especially the outdoor variety—is also related to the *chata* culture, as discussed in Chapter 5. During the Communist era, *chatas* were the only private property that Czechs were allowed to have. They took enormous pride in transforming their *chatas* into their own personal retreats, almost always using scavenged materials and a healthy dose of ingenuity. That affection continues today, and as we have seen many Czechs enjoy DIY activities and gardening when on their little plots of land. Anything grown on this land is likely to be used by the family as fresh produce and for canning—such as homemade jams and pickles. If a visitor receives a homemade gift, it is to be treasured!

Perhaps it is also the love of the outdoors that motivates the Czech love of dogs. In Prague especially it is easy to get the feeling that the size of pet dogs is in inverse proportion to the size of the apartment in which the animals live. But small living quarters or no, it is impossible to imagine Prague without its immense population of pampered pooches (or attendant dog messes, which the law requires to be cleaned up but are most often left for unsuspecting pedestrians). Visitors who are allergic or who have any fear of large dogs would be well-advised to avoid parks, but as in many other European cities, dogs will be found almost everywhere—from restaurants to shops to streets. Still, Prague dogs are on the whole a well-behaved lot, and the obvious Czech affection for them speaks loudly to Czechs' generous hearts.

CULTURE VULTURES

Of course, not all Czechs spend their free time taking their huge dogs on grueling hikes in the mountains. Given the vibrant Czech cultural scene, especially in Prague and other urban areas, Czechs are spoiled for choice when it comes to museums, concerts, and theater.

Prague boasts two national opera companies, several major orchestras, countless theaters and concert houses, and more galleries and museums than could be seen in a year's time—and the Czechs are justifiably proud of their offerings. Although many people complain about the tourist-inspired ticket pricing at some of the most well-known venues, Czechs can still find a good deal on tickets for most events. (Visitors are unlikely to be able to share in these prices, but compared to most major North American urban centers, tickets for cultural events will seem inexpensive.)

Certain cultural events in Prague are on offer primarily for the benefit of tourists, and you are unlikely to find any locals at these. Concerts by "A Famous Orchestra" featuring "Well-known Soloists" or performers in period dress are strictly for tourist consumption. While the performance may well be competent, keep in mind that the city offers truly outstanding performances, usually at a fraction of the price, in state-owned venues such as the Národní divadlo (National Theater) or Rudolfinum (home of the Czech Philharmonic). Still, for visitors in July and August, tourist concerts may be the only way to take in some musical culture since many national stages are dark during the summer. In any case, Czechs would likely be at their *chatas*.

The best place for an English speaker to find times and venues for cultural offerings is the supplement to the weekly newspaper, the *Prague Post.* The "Night and Day" section has a helpful array of not only concerts, gallery openings, and nightlife but also a spread of restaurant reviews and ratings. The paper comes out on Wednesday afternoons and is available at most newsstands in the city center.

SHOPPING: THE NEW LEISURE ACTIVITY

Given the dearth of attractive shopping options available to Czechs before 1989, it's not too surprising that the idea of shopping as a pastime took a few years to catch on. But caught on it has, and the Czechs now love their malls, hypermarkets, and box stores. When Swedish furniture and lifestyle retailer IKEA opened its first Czech store on the outskirts of Prague in 1996, more than 100,000 people showed up for the first four days of business. That's nearly 8 percent of Prague residents.

More recently, when the British electronics giant Dixon inaugurated an electronics superstore in 2003, there was a six-mile traffic jam leading to the store and reports of near-riot conditions among the masses of approximately 10,000 people—many of whom had slept outside overnight to be among the first allowed in the store—looking to take advantage of the advertised bargains on what are usually pricey electronic goods.

Malls are now commonplace and can be crowded during peak shopping times. Many have multiplexes and grocery stores as anchors and are therefore widely utilized across large swathes of the population. In smaller cities, malls have still not reached the same level of popularity, but big box stores such as the British retailer Tesco and French grocery chain Carrefour attract crowds throughout the week.

While such shopping centers do indeed feature many ordinary Czechs at leisure, the level of interest for the average visitor is limited. Shopping for clothes or other "mall" goods is inadvisable in the Czech Republic, as such items tend to be expensive compared to North America and Britain and quality and selection lower as well. Moreover, the goods of most interest to visitors—tourist items such as crystal or garnets—are available in greater variety in the center.

Still, for a visitor craving a taste of home, a shopping center like Novy Smichov at the Andel metro stop or Palác Flora at the Flora stop will provide the necessary if somewhat surreal experience of Western mass retailing that may be required. And as movies are generally run in the original language with Czech subtitles, taking in a big Hollywood blockbuster at the multiplex while there could provide the finishing touches on a homesickness prevention program.

SIGHT-SEEING

The vast majority of visitors to the Czech Republic—most of whom are likely to spend most if not all of their time in Prague—probably do not stay long enough to need a fix of Middle America. Besides, Prague's many other attractions should definitely rate higher on the priority list than a trip to the movies.

Any competent guidebook can lead a visitor through the "big" spots of Prague, which include Malá Strana, the Charles Bridge, and the castle (Pražský hrad); Old Town Square (Staroměstské Náměstí) and the Jewish Quarter; and Wenceslas Square (Václavské Náměstí) and New Town (Nové město). It would also be easy to follow the crowd from spot to spot.

But with ten centuries of history behind it, Prague can offer something different for every visitor, even if the sites might be the same.

Prague Castle

Prague Castle has been the official and unofficial seat of Czech power since the ninth century. Today, it houses the offices of the president and is thought to be the largest castle area in the world. It is also the most visited site in Prague. Visitors buy a group ticket to several attractions, and the ticket is good for three days from purchase.

History buffs will want to pay special attention to the site of the famous Prague defenestration in the Council Room of the Old Royal Palace. Literature lovers can stop by Number 22 on the Golden Lane. Franz Kafka lived here in the early twentieth century and worked on several of his stories. As in most of the tiny dwellings on the lane, Number 22 now houses a small specialty shop, but it is not hard to imagine Kafka crafting his intricate and bizarre stories within the walls of the castle when tourists did not rule the spread.

 St. Vitus Cathedral, the silhouette of which tops one of the most famous views in Prague, is well worth a visit, especially for art lovers. The stained glass windows in the cathedral were largely completed in the early twentieth century with money from patrons that included the most powerful business interests of the day. Even noted Czech artist Alfons Mucha, best-known for his art posters, completed a window in the cathedral. It is immediately recognizable for its use of paint on glass rather than soldered pieces. There is also a newly restored mosaic on the outside of the cathedral facing the royal palace that should not be missed.

To avoid the crowds and tables of tourist junk on the main steps, it is possible to descend the castle area through the Palace Gardens, which lead to a small square and museum. The gardens are beautiful and peaceful, offering spectacular views of the city. There is a small charge, but the vistas and solitude may well be worth it. Alternatively, walk back through the castle to the exit leading toward Úvoz/Nerudova Street and enjoy a stop for tea at Cajovna U Zeleného caje, which was featured in the 1988 Miloš Forman film *Amadeus*. (Teahouses have recently become very popular among Czechs, and the variety and quality of teas available may surprise visitors.)

Beyond the castle area, Malá Strana (which translates awkwardly to Lesser Quarter) has much to offer sightseers. Taking the funicular up Petřín hill and walking down is a delightful way to spend an afternoon, and the fare is only the cost of a normal public transportation ticket. Many Czechs often make the trip up the hill to visit the observatory or to test their athletic skills with a climb to the top of the Petřín "Eiffel Tower."

Malá Strana links with Old Town via the Charles Bridge, perhaps the most-famous single tourist attraction in Prague. The picturesque fourteenth-century bridge accommodates only foot traffic now, and there is a constant fear that its popularity may be its undoing. For several years the  Czech government and the Prague city government have tried to devise ways of doing needed repairs on the bridge—which was built in 1357 and is held together in part with eggs—but there is literally no time of day or night or season of the year in which the bridge is not used. Still, the bridge survived the disastrous floods of 2002 with little damage, so the eggs must be doing something right.

Old Town and the Jewish Quarter
The center of Prague's Old Town is the beautifully preserved Staroměstské Náměstí (Old Town Square). One of the few completely authentic Old Town centers in Europe, Prague's Old Town was untouched during the Second World War, and its towering spires and churches create an unmistakable feeling of history.

The best way to see Old Town (and, for that matter, much of the rest of Prague) is simply to

walk around and explore the tiny side streets and passages. The entire Old Town area can be easily taken in on foot, and although public transportation is available, things are so close as to make the local connections unnecessary. In the square itself, top attractions include the Orloj astronomical clock on the Old Town Hall (its figures emerge on the hour, and crowds gather in advance of the "event" to get a good spot); the Old Town Hall itself, including the tower climb for an amazing view of the city, and the Jan Hus statue (the text reads

"Love the Truth. Let others have their truth and truth will prevail.").

There are also things to avoid in Old Town, chief among them the restaurants and sidewalk cafés in the square. Overpriced and mediocre at best, the establishments on the square may have a nice view, but the view won't make up for the feeling you will get of being ripped off. In addition, sitting at an outdoor café in Old Town Square is an excellent place to have a purse or wallet stolen by one of the many petty criminals who prey on wowed tourists. (See the section on security in Chapter 7 for more information.) Extra vigilance can pay off here.

The Jewish Quarter, or Josefov, is the other star attraction of Old Town and is well worth a visit, despite the hordes of tourists who descend on the small venues every day. Prague has a well-preserved Jewish Quarter for a macabre reason. During the Nazi occupation, Hitler chose Prague's center of Jewish life—which in its heyday was home to as many as 35,000 Jews, who were among the most affluent and assimilated in Europe and included such notables as Kafka and, for a while, Albert Einstein—to serve as a "Museum of an Extinct Race" after he deported the vast majority of its residents. The Nazis painstakingly preserved and catalogued thousands of items of Jewish everyday life so that future generations would be able to learn about the people whom Hitler had ordered exterminated.

Today, the collection—housed in several buildings and synagogues—has been augmented with heart-wrenching exhibits about the children of the concentration camp Terezín and other information about the Holocaust.

Visitors to the quarter who wish to see the exhibits and the famous Old Jewish Cemetery—where more than 100,000 people are buried, in as many as twelve layers—must buy a collective ticket to the entire museum. The ticket is not cheap, but the museum is well translated in English, and the management does a decent job of timing visitors so that the venues remain accessible and viewable even during peak times. In short, despite the expense and crowds, this is one tourist spot that really shouldn't be missed. Arriving early in the morning or late in the afternoon can be the best way to beat the hordes.

New Town and Wenceslas Square
It may not be readily apparent today given the enormous neon signs and touts accosting visitors to go to strip bars, but Václavské Náměstí

(Wenceslas Square) has been the site of amazing events for the Czech Republic, and as the center of Nové město (New Town) merits a look. Wenceslas himself surveys the square on horseback from the top of the square, and if someone in Prague tells you to meet "at the horse," this statue is what he or she means.

In 1918, the First Republic of Czechoslovakia was declared here on Wenceslas Square. In 1968, Soviet tanks opened fire on the National Museum at the top of the square to crush the Prague Spring uprising. More than twenty years later, the Czechs won the day when hundreds of thousands of people gathered in the square to protest against the Communist regime, ultimately toppling the government.

Today, most of the toppling on Wenceslas Square seems to involve rowdy British youths celebrating stag parties by falling over drunk, but the kilometer-long boulevard is still worth a walk. As with Old Town Square, it's best to avoid the restaurants and cafés directly on the square, but there are good dining possibilities just off it on the side streets. And a word about the "nightclubs" incessantly advertised on the square: In Prague, there is only one meaning of the word "nightclub," and it is not a social gathering place for young people to dance. It's a brothel. Prostitution is not legal but is largely tolerated in the Czech capital.

It's also best to be an extremely wary pedestrian on the square—cars are still allowed and drivers remain relatively unconcerned about the safety of people on foot, although there are plans in the works to pedestrianize the entire area.

Visitors may also encounter shady types offering to change money on the street. It's hard to believe that these people still fool enough tourists to make their venture worthwhile, but there must still be enough gullible people around. Don't be one of them. (See Chapter 7 for more information about changing money safely.)

Other New Town attractions worth a trip include Vyšehrad—the legendary home of the Přemsylid dynasty—the Mucha Museum, which houses an impressive collection of original and poster work by the famous artist Alfons Mucha, and the Art Nouveau masterpiece Municipal House (Obecní dům) near Náměstí republiky (Republic Square).

EATING AND DRINKING

Restaurants and pubs are extremely popular in the Czech capital, and not just among tourists. Moreover, the dining scene has exploded in the last decade. A few short years ago, it was hard to find restaurants that served much beyond *pivo* (beer) and *vepřo, knedlo, zelo* (roast pork with dumplings and sauerkraut). Now, nearly every kind of cuisine—from vegetarian to traditional meat-and-potatoes to ethnic staples to four-star—is available in Prague.

Czech food is covered in the next section, but there are specific customs and expectations visitors should be aware of when dining or drinking out. In choosing a restaurant or pub, it is wise to first check the menu posted outside. Nearly all establishments will have a menu available under glass just outside the door, and those that don't are probably best avoided as rip-offs. Once inside, it is customary to wait to be seated, and the waiter should bring menus before any orders are made. Menus in English are common in the center, and  sometimes waiters will ask which language is preferred. Beware of establishments that try to make you order without seeing a menu, as prices are often inflated for foreigners.

Wait staff will first take drink orders and do not take kindly to patrons trying to order food at that point. Soups, salads, entrées, and side dishes are sold separately in most places, so if you want dumplings with your goulash, don't forget to ask for them. You will almost certainly be prompted to choose your *přílohy* (side dish), but don't think that it is included in the meal. It will appear separately on your check.

Waiters often use a chicken-scratch-like hash mark system to keep track of what you're eating and drinking. It can be almost impossible for a visitor to figure out what the marks indicate, and the mental math that most wait staff engage in to find your total can be hard to verify. Restaurants are required by law to present you with a formal check printed from a cash register, so don't be afraid to ask for an *účet* (check), especially if you think your mental math and that of your waiter don't match. It is sadly very common for restaurant staff to take advantage of tourists by adding on extra beers or unordered bread, for example, and visitors should not be intimidated about insisting on a full accounting.

Some restaurants and pubs will charge *couvert*, a cover charge for the table, bread, and condiments. Although this is legal, any restaurant charging it must state so on the menu. If your check comes back with *couvert* that you did not expect, you can ask to have it removed. Success is not guaranteed, but it is within your rights.

TIPPING

Tipping customs are changing as the restaurant scene does, but 10 percent is appropriate for visitors in all but the most formal or grimy establishments. A Czech would be likely to simply round up his or her check by a few crowns, but foreigners are expected to give more. Tips are presented when paying the check by telling the waitperson how much you would like to pay (not, crucially, how much you would like to get back). For example, if the check is 400 crowns and you have a 1000-crown note and would like to pay 450 crowns, be sure to say 450, not 550 for the change. Otherwise, you will have given an extremely generous if unanticipated tip. Don't leave tips on the table.

In a cab tips are not expected, but it is customary to round up the fare.

Separate checks are easily accommodated in most places, and a cashier (usually a member of the wait staff but not always) will visit your table to tally things up. You will generally be asked if you want to pay together (*dohromady)* or separately (*zvlášť')*. If paying separately, be prepared to recite what you ordered, including number of drinks.

One more thing to keep in mind: wait staff will not bring a check to your table automatically. One of the nice things about dining in the Czech Republic (and in most of the rest of Europe) is that there is no pressure to get in and out quickly. A waiter may visit your table only once or twice in a meal to get drink refills or dessert orders— never to pressure you to vacate the space. If you want your check, ask for it by saying, *Zaplatíme, prosím* (We'll pay now, please) or *Účet, prosím* (Check, please).

CZECH FOOD
Many people have no idea what to expect from Czech food, as there are very few Czech restaurants outside of the Czech Republic— certainly not like more familiar cuisines such as Italian, Mexican, or Chinese!

Czech food tends to be hearty, filling, and rich. Many of the ingredients are basic—pork, potatoes, cabbage—but the end result can be delicious, if you're in the mood. The Czech national dish is probably the roast pork, dumplings, and sauerkraut platter mentioned in the previous section, but there are also other perennial favorites worth trying.

Svíčková na smetaně is beef sirloin roast in a succulent sweet cream sauce, served over *knedliky* (bread dumplings, a Czech staple) and topped with a lemon slice, a dollop of whipped cream, and tart berries. There is no middle ground on *Svíčková*—you'll either love it or hate it. Czech *guláš* (goulash) is much maligned by fans of the Hungarian version—it definitely has far less kick— but is a fairly reliable staple of the Czech kitchen. Chunks of beef in more or less spicy sauce over bread dumplings, *guláš* is a safe choice for most visitors.

Meat *řízek*—generally pork or chicken breast—is the Czech answer to Wiener schnitzel, the pounded, egg-dipped, and breaded cutlet for which Vienna is famous. The Czech version is somewhat smaller and is often served with *hranolky* (French fries) or *americké brambory* (potato wedges—called American potatoes in Czech). Vegetarians will always have the uniquely Czech offer of *smažený sýr* (fried cheese)—a breaded, deep-fried hunk of either mild white cheese or the Czech equivalent of Camembert, called Hermelin—served with French fries and *tatarky* (tartar sauce). Good for your arteries? Probably not. Good for your soul? Definitely.

Soup is much loved in Czech cuisine, with *bramboračka* (hearty, sometimes spicy potato soup) and *kulajda* (cold sour soup with dill and potatoes) serving as particular national favorites. Soup orders are likely to be accompanied by a basket of *šumava* (dense wheat-rye bread) and *rohlík* (crusty, tube-shaped white bread rolls). Common desserts include *jablečný zavín* (apple strudel) and *palačinky* (crêpes), usually served with fruit or ice cream or both.

The average Czech would be likely to have only one "hot" meal per day, usually lunch. Breakfast is a very light meal, maybe just *rohlíky* and coffee or tea, perhaps with some yogurt. (The concept of weekend brunch is also catching on.) Taking a short break in the mid-morning for a light snack (*svačina*)—often something sweet such as a pastry—and coffee is not uncommon. The evening meal is usually nothing more elaborate than some hearty *šumava* bread and cheese or meat. It's completely acceptable to have beer at lunch—even at most business lunches— but *mineralka* (mineral water) or soft drinks are common as well.

Fresh fruits and vegetables are not overly common in restaurants (except when deep-fried or in dessert), but excellent produce is available when in season at fruit and vegetable markets around town. While Czechs don't have as wide a year-round selection of fruits and vegetables as people in North America are used to, the produce they do have tastes much better because it's in season and relatively local. Once you've had a perfectly ripe Czech strawberry in May or June or a juicy peach in August, you won't want to eat the fruit at your local grocery store ever again.

chapter seven

TRAVEL, HEALTH, & SECURITY

Getting into the Czech Republic is easy for most North Americans and Europeans. Until the Czech Republic joined the European Union in May 2004, Canadians had to get visas to enter the country, but that restriction was lifted to bring the country in line with existing E.U. visa norms.

To enter the country for stays shorter than ninety days, visitors need only present a passport, but it must be valid for at least six months beyond the date of entry. This restriction is nonnegotiable, and there is every chance that you could be prevented from boarding the plane in your country of origin. Make sure to check your passport before you plan a trip. Visitors may also be asked to present proof of ongoing travel before they board the plane or pass through customs, either in the form of a round-trip airline/train/bus ticket or a ticket to somewhere outside of the Czech Republic. However, being asked for this would be unusual for a visitor from Western Europe or North America.

Those visitors not planning to stay in "commercial" accommodations such as hotels or hostels are required by law to register themselves with the Foreigners' Police, within three business days of arrival. (Anyone staying in a commercial facility will be registered by the facility.) As a practical matter, however, many tourists ignore this law— mostly out of ignorance of the statute—and it is rarely enforced. Still, anyone wishing to be entirely correct and law-abiding can visit the appropriate office of the Foreigners' Police at Sdružení 1, Prague 4, by taking the red (C) metro line to Pankrác.

MONEY

The best and perhaps only recommended way to change your home currency into crowns is to withdraw them from one of the many ATMs that dot the city. ATMs are easily located in all arrival areas—the airport, train stations, and even border crossings—and will provide visitors the prevailing exchange rate without any fees beyond that of the ATM and the bank. It's a good idea to check with your home bank before you leave to

find out what kind of fees they have for
withdrawing money overseas and to make sure
their ATM network is represented in the country
(most are).

Paying with credit cards at the point of sale is
more possible in Czech cities than in many
German ones, for example, but it's not as easy as
in North America. Establishments accepting
credit cards will have the familiar stickers on the
front doors, but it is smart to ask before you buy
or order anything to make sure that cards are
accepted. Some places will also not offer their
best "deal" to those paying with credit cards, as it
requires both a fee paid on their part and a record
of the transaction for the tax police. It's also a
good idea to check if your credit card company
charges a foreign transaction fee—many charge
as much as 2 to 3 percent of the total transaction,
and that fee is often buried in fine print.

Even with fees, however, paying with credit
cards and withdrawing money using ATM/debit
cards is always a better deal than exchanging cash
or travelers' checks. There is an entire cottage
industry of money-changers devoted to fleecing
tourists out of as much cash as possible when
doing currency exchanges—and this is true even
for the commercial exchange facilities that dot
the tourist districts. Although all such
establishments are required to post their rates

outside their stores, most show prominently only the "sell" rates—the rate the office is giving to people exchanging crowns for dollars or euros, not the other way around.

If you absolutely must change currency in Prague, do so at an internationally reputable establishment such as American Express or Thomas Cook, or a bank. While they may not offer the best-looking rate, the fees are reasonable and there are no hidden catches such as lower rates for smaller transactions. And it should go without saying that you should never, ever change money on the street. To do so is not only illegal but also potentially dangerous—leaving you open to theft—and will likely leave you with worthless Bulgarian or Polish currency.

PUBLIC TRANSPORTATION

Prague is a very easy city to get around via public transportation. Its system is efficient, inexpensive, and clean, and most visitors will be able to master the basics in just a few hours. There are three subway lines that make up the Metro, A (green), B (yellow), and C (red). The lines link up at the Florenc, Můstek, and Muzeum central stations for transfers. In addition to the subway, there is an extensive network of streetcars and buses. Most visitors, unless they are staying at a remote hotel or hostel, will primarily depend on streetcars and the metro.

Schedules are posted at the stops for buses and streetcars , and the metro comes at regular intervals (more frequently during busy times on weekdays) that are sometimes posted on schedules at the station. Central stations have countdown clocks on large television screens, and every metro station has a clock at the end of the tunnel to tell you how long it's been since the last train.

Tickets for public transportation are affordable and universal—with one ticket, it's possible to ride the buses, streetcars, metro, and even the funicular at Petřín. To determine what type of

ticket you'll need, look at the number of stops you'll need to make. A single ticket (currently 8 crowns) covers a simple journey of no more than fifteen minutes on a bus or streetcar or no more than four stops on the metro.

Anything more complicated requires a transfer ticket that stands today at 12 crowns. For simplicity's sake, it may be easier to buy a long-term ticket, which will cover all journeys for twenty-four hours, three days, seven days, or fifteen days. All tickets must be validated before first use (by sticking them into the yellow day/time/route punchers that are found at the entrance to every metro station and on the buses and streetcars).

Tickets are available for purchase in stations from the orange and yellow machines (with coins—none take bills), from Tabak stores, and in some convenience shops and hotels. If you're not buying an extended pass, it's smart to buy a few tickets of the two denominations at one stop so that you don't find yourself at 11:00 p.m. with no change and nowhere open to buy a ticket. (You should also be aware that the regular system closes at midnight, although there are night streetcars and buses.)

On that note, as tempting as it might be, never ride public transportation in Prague without a ticket. It's true that you can walk right on to the system without showing proof of purchase, but there is a very active band of plainclothes ticket enforcers who are on the lookout at all times for people—especially tourists—without proper fare. This is true even on the bus from the airport!

It is very, very common to be "enforced" while on public transportation. The inspector will show his or her badge, and the rider must show his or her ticket. If a valid ticket cannot be produced, the rider will be escorted off public transportation and made to pay a fine. Do not expect tourist ignorance to get you anywhere with these inspectors. They have heard every story, and most speak English. The fines are not huge but are in most cases more than even a monthly transit pass. Moreover, although it's possible to hear people— especially longtime Praguers—boast about never buying a ticket and never getting caught, such largesse just doesn't extend to tourists. And in any case, a system like Prague's doesn't run without money: it seems immoral to take advantage of an offering as extensive, reasonably priced, and well-run as the Prague public transportation.

TAXIS

Speaking of immoral, the situation surrounding taxis in Prague has prompted government intervention at the highest municipal level. It is unfortunately all too common for taxi drivers to "take their fares for rides" in the rip-off sense of the phrase. Throughout Prague's center, idling taxis line the streets waiting for unsuspecting tourists to ask to be taken somewhere. While there is no physical danger in hailing a cab on the street—beyond the normal risk of the appalling way most drive—there is a great financial risk. Such street taxis very often lack meters, and even those with meters may have installed devices to make them run at higher-than-legal speeds. A trip

that should cost just 100 crowns or thereabouts
might end up costing several times that.

The Prague City government has been working
for years—with undercover inspectors, fine
structures, and other legal remedies—to try to
combat this problem, but the bottom line for
visitors is that the only way to be sure of not
getting ripped off is to use one of the reputable
"radio" taxis, such as AAA, Profi, or Halo.
(Current numbers are always
listed in the *Prague Post*.)
All three services have
English-speaking operators
available and will dispatch a
car with an easily verifiable

number on the side to pick you up. You can even
negotiate the price in advance. It's worth it to ask
for one of these three services by name, even if
you are having a hotel or restaurant call for you.
Many hotels and restaurants have kickback deals
with alternative transportation companies, and the
emphasis is not on a fair deal for customers but
on the profit margin.

At the airport, there is a monopoly of Visa
taxis and cargo vans (people carriers) with fixed-
price services. It is perfectly safe to take these
taxis, although you will certainly pay more for
the individual transport in the Visa cars than if
you were to call AAA to pick you up at the end of

the terminal. (It should be noted that the Visa taxis, ironically, do not take credit cards!) The group vans can be a good option if you're not in a hurry to get to your accommodation as they will drop off as many as ten people in one trip.

RENTING A CAR

Anyone planning to visit Prague exclusively during a visit to the Czech Republic should not bother with a rental car. Parking is horrendous and driving fast-paced and dangerous—definitely not worth the hassle!

Many day trips can be done easily with long-distance public transportation such as trains or buses, but for some overnight stays or for places really off the beaten path, renting a car is a viable option. Car rentals on the spur of the moment can be arranged through the state travel agency, Čedok, or at American Express. It can be more expensive than in the United States, and gas will certainly set you back more, but the flexibility it provides can be worth it. In fact, many long-term foreign residents of the Czech Republic rent cars occasionally rather than own one because of the hassle of ownership.

One advance rental option with easy

e-mail and Web options is Rentpoint
(http://www.rentpoint.cz/en/index.html). They
have fair prices, weekend specials, drop-off and
pickup services, and English-speaking staff.

TRAINS AND BUSES

Czech Railways and its related in-country bus
service runs efficiently and conveniently. Local
tickets are also quite reasonably priced—
buses even more so than trains. The least
intimidating way to learn about rail
options in Prague is to visit the main
Čedok office on Na příkopě. English-
speaking clerks can guide you through
the process of finding schedules and
buying tickets, regardless of destination.

For the more adventurous, the IDOS
Web site's English pages (http://www.idos.cz)
offer ready, if not immediately understandable,
access to all train and bus schedules, and tickets
can be purchased without much hassle at train
and bus stations throughout the country.

Before embarking, try to find out where the
bus or train will deposit you in your place of
destination. Even in some tourist centers, the bus
and/or train stations aren't centrally located, so
you'll want to have an idea of how to get to the
main attractions from the drop-off point.

WALKING

The best way to get around within cities and towns is often on foot. Prague's main sites are within walking distance of each other, and distances are much closer than they appear on maps. As mentioned in the previous chapter, it's important to be a vigilant pedestrian when crossing streets—a law passed in 2000 mandates that cars stop at pedestrian crossings, but the net result of the law was a 100 percent rise in pedestrian fatalities—but other than that, walking is a great way to see the city.

Of course, supportive and comfortable walking shoes will be a great asset—many visitors find that the uneven cobblestone streets can be hard on feet and ankles, and given the general state of Prague sidewalks, finding oneself sprawled across the pavement is no fun. Outside of Prague, most cities and small towns will have an easily walkable center, probably even a pedestrian zone, so walking is advised there as well.

And if you want to be a pedestrian throughout the country? Hitchhiking between cities is a common and legal way for Czech soldiers and students to get around and is generally safe. Those looking for rides congregate near highways carrying signs sporting their desired destination, and most riders will offer gas money—although it may or may not be accepted.

A WORD ABOUT ACCESSIBILITY

For the mobility-impaired, Prague is no picnic. Stairs line the entrances to most metro stations, streetcars require steep steps up, and uneven cobblestone streets can make travel hazardous. There are a few metro stations with elevators and several handicapped-accessible buses, but overall it's a difficult city for those who require a wheelchair or have other special needs. Several nonprofit groups have been trying to pressure the Czech government to improve the city's accessibility, but in a country undergoing economic transition, it hasn't been a priority.

Disabled visitors who ask will receive help from ordinary Czechs on the street in terms of getting into and out of public transportation and navigating the city. Don't be afraid to ask for help (*pomoc*) as people really are used to assisting others, even if their bland public-transportation demeanor doesn't reveal it.

FINDING YOUR WAY

For most visitors, a general Prague map with an enlarged inset of the center will be sufficient for basic navigation. However, for those who may want to get out of downtown or who have business in the country that requires travel to out-of-the-way places, the best resource is an Internet site called Mapy.cz. Although it has no English pages, the process is fairly self-explanatory. Enter the name and number of the address you are looking for into the blank box (diacritics are not important) and choose the city you need to search in. The site will find the address on a scaleable, printable map, and the map also lists nearby public transportation stops.

Addresses in Czech will be written with street first, followed by one or two numbers. The postal code will tell you which district of Prague the address is in. For example, the Mucha Museum is located at Panská 7, 110 00 Prague. The district in the Prague postal code is indicated by the second number, so in this case, the museum is located in Prague's first district, the historic center of town. The city is divided into ten main districts, although most travelers will spend the bulk of their time in Prague 1. You may notice that there are two numbers on the buildings in Prague, a red number and a blue number. The blue number (called an orientation number, *číslo orientační*) is the one that is important as it represents the familiar sequential house number known in most European cities. The red numbers (descriptive number or *číslo popisne*) may not be concurrent with adjacent buildings as it describes only the buildings in a particular section of town—the streets of which can cross in seemingly nonsensical ways. If both numbers are written in an address, the red number will be first, but you should search for the blue number.

Sooner or later it is almost inevitable that you will find yourself lost in Prague. The streets are narrow and often not parallel, and it's easy to get turned around without a street sign in sight. It is almost always safe to ask for directions on the street, and shopkeepers are usually willing to help as well. In recent years the city of Prague has tried to put more beat cops on patrol downtown, and they can generally help lost visitors as well. Getting lost can even be a good thing—there are so many hidden passages and tiny alleyways in Prague that it's sometimes the best way to stumble onto something wonderful.

SECURITY

Unfortunately for Prague tourism officials—and indeed, for legions of unlucky tourists—Prague has acquired a not entirely undeserved reputation as a hotbed of petty crime. While there are very few neighborhoods in which it is dangerous to walk at night or where a visitor might be in actual physical danger, the chances of getting robbed or pick-pocketed in broad daylight are not inconsequential.

There are some prime locations for such crimes to take place—the metro and streetcars, crowded tourist spots such as Old Town Square, and busy restaurants—as well as perennial schemes that seem to happen again and again, including being surrounded and having pockets and purses rifled by several large men and the rustling newspaper or map distraction on a crowded train. The gangs that perpetrate these thefts have made a virtual art form of their attacks, and many people don't even realize they've been robbed until they reach for their wallet at some later time.

It's not only visitors to Prague who are victims, either. Ordinary Czechs and longtime foreign residents are just as likely to fall prey. The best way to protect yourself is to be vigilant almost to the point of paranoia. A money belt worn under your clothes is the best way to carry cash, credit cards, and identity documentation. Once you've reached your accommodation, ask about a safe for your valuables, and never carry your passport with you, unless you feel that your accommodation is unsafe. (Foreigners are required to have their passports with them, but a photocopy of the first page will suffice.) If you must carry a purse, make it one with a strap that you can attach to your body and to an item of furniture at any restaurant or café stops you might make. Wallets should never be carried in back pockets—and even front pockets are not completely safe. Never keep valuables in coat pockets when you hang up your jacket in a restaurant or café.

If you should find yourself a victim of crime, you can report it to the police and may get some sympathy and an exotic-looking police report, but you are unlikely to recover your stolen possessions. You should find out from your credit card companies if a police report is required, however. The police department should provide a translator, although it may take a while. If you lose your passport, be sure to go straight to your embassy or consulate as it can take time to gather the necessary documentation to have it replaced. Having a copy of your important documents in a separate location and at home with a trusted friend or family member can aid in this process.

HEALTH MATTERS

There are no special vaccinations or health concerns when considering travel to the Czech Republic. Tap water is almost always safe—although it may not taste great in some places—

and the standard of medical care is high.

It is important to check that any medical insurance you have will cover travel within the Czech Republic. E.U. citizens are covered by reciprocal agreements, but most hospitals will require non-E.U. foreigners (especially U.S. citizens) to pay for medical care upfront. Prague has several "foreigner" medical clinics and even a foreigners' hospital section at Na Homolce. The *Prague Post* lists the contact information for all such facilities in its weekly "Night and Day" section.

WHERE TO STAY

Accommodations tend to be basic but clean. They are no longer a bargain in the Czech Republic, especially in Prague and especially in high season. Expect to pay only slightly less for a hotel in Prague than you would in a major Western European city. Hostels are still a good deal for budget travelers, although they fill up quickly, and in the summer making reservations is not just recommended but mandatory.

The neighborhood you choose is much less important than its proximity to public transportation. Prices for downtown accommodations are higher than those in the suburbs, and if you find a place outside the center with good public transportation links, it can be just as convenient. When making a choice, be sure to ask how far it is to the nearest metro or streetcar stop and whether you will have to ride multiple forms of transportation to get to the center. Accommodations may not be a bargain if you have to ride an hour each way to get to the center. Remember that normal public transportation closes at midnight and the night streetcars won't necessarily go your way!

Star ratings are not necessarily indicative of what you will find, since they are not awarded by any regulated body. Still, most accommodation options are likely to be basic but clean.

For longer stays, it can make sense to rent an apartment. There are numerous agencies and private owners who rent out apartments; one of the most reliable is Mary's (http://www.marys.cz). It's also worth checking out expats.cz for short-term sublets or apartment shares.

chapter eight

BUSINESS BRIEFING

Czech business culture has changed extensively since the fall of Communism. Today it is a mixture of post-Communist transitional practices, the legacies of the Habsburg and Soviet empires, and newly introduced Western business norms. For foreigners who come to conduct business for a few days or longer there are certain guidelines worth knowing about. Having the inside track can be extremely beneficial at the negotiating table or when signing a contract.

TIMING A VISIT

When planning a business trip to the Czech Republic, remember that there are definite times of the year, and even the week, to avoid. Scheduling a meeting anytime after lunch on Friday is a nonstarter. Weekends start early in the Czech Republic, especially when the weather is nice. Friday evening business meetings or weekend events are almost unheard of and therefore a bad idea.

The summer in general is a terrible time to try to get any business done, as vacations are lengthy and workers unapologetic about taking them. From mid-June to September 1, expect long absences, which can mean that before one key decision maker has returned, another will depart. Since Czechs are very conscious of paperwork and procedure, trying to cut corners by having one person sign off on something for which they do not technically have responsibility—an administrative assistant, for example—or even to deal with an absence electronically, by fax or e-mail, is unlikely to be successful.

The Czechs in this regard are no different from most other Europeans—summer vacation is taken seriously across the Continent—but it is important for those coming from vacation-starved countries such as the United States to understand the situation before making plans.

It also makes sense to check the general holiday calendar (see Chapter 3) to avoid scheduling a trip over a Czech national holiday. Although many international offices are open on state holidays, work on such days is strictly voluntary, and many workers take not only the holiday off but also a few weekdays around it as well. The Christmas-to-New Year season in particular, as we have seen, is a time of very little work—except for wrapping up the fiscal year, which ends on December 31—and so also represents a bad time to plan a business trip.

In terms of time of day, you may find that your Czech colleagues want to start meetings at exceedingly early hours. The Czechs like early morning meetings, and many people start their workdays before 8:00 a.m. in order to be able to leave earlier in the afternoons. Some contend the Czech propensity for early rising is rooted in the Austro-Hungarian empire, because Emperor Franz Josef II suffered from insomnia and so started his business day at 6:00 a.m., a practice eventually adopted by the wider population.

PREPARING FOR BUSINESS

Once a business trip has been scheduled, preparation should begin. While going to the Czech Republic does not require much in the way of passports, visas, or inoculations for most people, it is worth asking about any customs regulations or attendant bureaucracy you may encounter well in advance, since navigating such seas requires considerable time.

Call in advance to set up times and places of meetings and begin serious investigations. Background research is hugely important, and should be conducted independently of the people you are planning to meet in the country. It's not that Czechs are untrustworthy, just that "both the government and the private sector operate under a different set of expectations, and to them what may appear as a unique business opportunity for foreigners may in fact not be so attractive when measured by foreign standards"—as one woman who worked for an international consulting firm in Prague told *Culture Smart!*

Beyond business research, it is key to find out what languages are going to be used in negotiations (see below for suggestions) and to determine if you need to arrange for your own interpreter or translator. Whatever the case, learning a few polite phrases in Czech will go a long way toward breaking the ice.

Checking the weather is also a good idea, as showing up drenched after a spring rain is not going to do much to help your credibility.

In planning your schedule, make sure to allow yourself plenty of time to get to the meeting. Punctuality is important to Czechs—while not as important as it is for Germans or Swiss—so every effort should be made to be on time. Traffic in Prague can be bad, especially from 8:00 a.m. onward, so if you're taking a cab, be sure to allot yourself extra time. If you will be taking public transportation or walking, making a trial run the night before is a good idea. If you do find yourself running late, it's best to call ahead as a courtesy.

INTRODUCTIONS AND GETTING STARTED

Compared with many American enterprises, the conduct of Czech business may seem quite formal. "Casual Fridays," for example, are not on the Czech radar. No matter what the day of the week, it is important to arrive dressed for the occasion—suits and ties for men, suits (with skirts if at all possible) for women.

At the initial meeting, it is customary to shake hands and exchange business cards. Business cards are extremely important and should clearly state your position and title, even if you are meeting colleagues from your own company. According to one foreign international finance executive, the quality of the printing and paper of the card is not crucially important—as it is in Japan, for example—but expect your card to be scrutinized for title and grade. If you are expected to manage people during your visit, it is important that your title makes it sound as if you have the power to do so. Hierarchy is important (more later), and you may need to "prove" your credentials with a business title. Your colleagues' business cards may in turn be helpful to you, particularly in figuring out how to spell the name of the person you are meeting.

Bringing gifts is not expected on a first meeting, although gifts and cards at Christmastime are expected for frequent business contacts and sometimes at second meetings. Gift-giving prohibitions or limits such as exist in the United States or Great Britain do not apply to Czech public officials, who are on the whole willing to accept gifts regardless of the possible appearance of favoritism or corruption.

After the exchange of business cards at an initial meeting, it is best to keep the conversation light. A Mexican international consultant interviewed for this book had this advice: "Make small talk, preferably about the sites to visit in the city, for example, and never go right to the main point to be covered in a first meeting. First meetings are left to create rapport, exchange business cards, and establish a working relationship."

A Scottish international bank executive had some additional words of wisdom for discussions at the first meeting: "Don't comment on the price of goods and remark how cheap everything is or how in your country everything is much better, larger, and so on. The Czech may do this themselves, but let them start the topic." A follow-up to that is not to get dragged into making such comparisons, even if your Czech colleagues do bring it up. Keep the tone light and complimentary.

Meetings can be held in or outside the office, although formal negotiations are most likely to take place in the office. Lunchtime restaurant meetings are very popular, and at any all-day meeting, a business lunch will be arranged. Much work and negotiations is, in fact, done over beers at the pub, but a foreigner—especially a woman— is unlikely to be privy to such discussions. For this reason, it is important to have a local partner to help you get the "real" story.

THE LANGUAGE BARRIER

Opinions vary as to which system works best for conducting business—hiring an interpreter, conducting business in English, or trying to keep it to Czech.

Here's one view, offered by the international consultant quoted earlier: "If you can conduct business in Czech, by all means use it. Whenever your Czech counterparts are allowed to speak in their native language, they will be more communicative and explicit. When they have to speak English, even if they do so fluently, they will become a lot more reserved and hesitant. On the other hand, if your Czech is not good enough, it is best to speak English. After a couple of serious grammatical errors or mistaken words, you will quickly lose respect, and it takes a lot of extra work to earn back that respect."

Given that most visitors are unlikely to speak Czech, the options narrow to uninterpreted or interpreted English, interpreted Czech, or simultaneous translation. If you decide to go with uninterpreted English because the bulk of people in the meeting seem to speak good English, remember to speak slowly and clearly, avoiding the use of slang. It is *very* uncommon for a Czech to admit that he or she has not understood something. If you ask as you go along if things are clear, the answer is almost always going to be yes, even when there may be misunderstandings. This is especially true among older Czech businessmen, who may have only fair language skills but are in charge of major decisions.

For this reason, the best scenario for a short-term visitor is probably simultaneous translation for both parties. An American private equity principal interviewed for this book admitted it is "a pain to have to go through an interpreter because you are never really sure that the exact message gets through," but the hassle of a third party is probably a better bet than worrying if important things are being completely misunderstood. The Scottish banker also emphasized the importance of finding an interpreter that you can trust, for example a lawyer from an international firm.

HIERARCHY AND SENIORITY

Figuring out who is "in charge" is generally not a problem. Hierarchy is extremely important, and most of the time the interior power structure will be apparent. As politically incorrect as it will sound to many North Americans, it is fairly safe to assume that the older male in the room is in charge until told differently. Business cards (number of titles if you can't read the actual job grade) can also be an important clue.

While observing basic rules of deference to authority—shaking hands first with the boss, directing as much eye contact as possible to that person, not questioning his or her authority in front of subordinates—visiting businesspeople may find that the harder part is gaining the respect of the Czechs with whom they are negotiating. With no selection of official professional titles to choose from, North Americans are at a disadvantage when it comes to proving their status. Making mention of one's qualifications may be necessary to establish one's credentials with Czech colleagues.

This is particularly true for foreign women. As one businesswoman said, "I noticed a terrible 'macho' mentality. There were very few women in leading positions within the business community. Men tended to be very rude to me and indifferent in initial meetings. I had to be abrasive and sharp in the first meetings in order to earn their respect. Many times I had to reference my previous work experience in order to assert my expertise." She added, however, that such experiences seemed to be a Europe-wide phenomenon, and Czechs were not necessarily the worst offenders.

There may be hidden conflicts within the organization that can make understanding the hierarchy difficult. These often revolve around expatriate/local differences, and between "entrenched" workers and those who embrace change. Directly after the fall of Communism, many companies brought in foreigners—many of whom had little or no experience of Czech business on the ground—to try to reform the business culture. These foreigners generally received handsome expatriate packages with much higher salaries and better benefits than the local workers. The system created considerable resentment toward expatriates and foreigners in general, which made working relationships difficult and upset the traditional hierarchies in place. The dichotomy is narrowing as more local people are put into management positions, but the legacy of distrust remains. Foreigners, even those who stay long-term, may feel shut out of business relationships.

In addition to the foreigner/local issue, in some organizations there may be a conflict between those who accept the changes brought about by the economic transition and those who would rather turn back the clock. The chasm that exists between those who embrace the "Westernization" of business and those who prefer the old Czech methods may not be apparent to you as a foreigner until you hit a brick wall. It may be the people at the top who are putting obstacles in the way of change. Even so, it is still important to be deferential—all the while finding a way to work more closely with those colleagues who see the possibilities inherent in change.

NEGOTIATING

Negotiation can be a lengthy process and is sure to be frustrating if it is not entered into with the right attitude. Expect things to take time, and don't expect negotiations to be conducted in an entirely straightforward manner. Many Czechs are not used to taking responsibility for decisions, and so can seem circuitous or even evasive. Red tape and bureaucratic hurdles are inevitable.

The best—and perhaps only—way to know what is actually going on at the table is to enlist the aid of a trusted local. As the Mexican consultant explained, "The strongest teams are always composed of foreign experts who can lead the way . . . together with the local partner who can explain the color and nuance of the operation." This is especially important for the out-of-office work sessions that tend to go on at the pub after work. After working for two years in an international firm in Prague, this consultant said that she would not have considered trying to conduct business in such a setting because of her status as a woman and a foreigner, so having a pair of eyes and ears in the pub was invaluable.

As regards the nuts and bolts of certain financial discussions, the international finance executive observed that in Czech business, all prices are negotiable because haggling is expected. In addition, he said, the cash price "is always cheaper" and negotiation of that is done verbally and in person, not via e-mail or postal mail.

When disagreements arise in negotiations, it is always best to try to solve them one-on-one outside the meeting, particularly if they involve a dispute that could challenge the authority of the boss. Given the Czechs' heightened sensitivity to status, such a direct confrontation in front of subordinates and/or colleagues could be so offensive as to derail the entire process.

REACHING AGREEMENT

If negotiations have been successfully concluded, expect considerable pomp and circumstance when it comes to signing contracts. The Czechs love contracts and paper trails, and especially affixing official stamps to their legal documents. The production and sale of these official stamps is quite limited, as is the number of people in a company who may legally use them. Management must file a list of senior executives who can sign and/or stamp official documents on behalf of the company. Expect to sign numerous copies on behalf of your enterprise as well, although you will of course lack an official stamp.

Maintaining an original, signed, stamped copy of any contracts concluded is crucial. Czechs do not recognize photocopies, unless they have been notarized, and sometimes not even then. (Being a notary is a full-time profession in the Czech Republic and is taken quite seriously. Anyone doing business is almost sure to need notary services at some point, and notaries can be found with relative ease throughout the city.)

In terms of contracts, it is important to verify which language used has legal standing. Sometimes both a Czech and an English contract will be produced, but the Czech contract can supercede the English one legally. Obviously, such an arrangement is not ideal. If at all possible, insist on an independent source to read and compare the contracts, or insist on a purely English contract.

Stamp-Happy

The Czech affection for rubber stamps forms the basis of one of the most famous scenes in Czech cinema. Jiří Menzel's 1966 New Wave masterpiece, *Closely Watched Trains*—based on the Bohumil Hrabal novel of the same name—won the 1967 Academy Award for Best Foreign Film and includes an unusual stamping scene, to say the least. One of the main characters, a libidinous middle-aged train dispatcher, uses official railway stamps to seduce a comely young telegraph operator, stamping her legs and backside over and over until she can't restrain herself any longer.

FULFILLMENT

In the case of ongoing projects, it is important to delineate responsibilities and expectations clearly. Tasks should be assigned to specific people, and the safest bet is to circulate a list of agreed-upon responsibilities to everyone involved shortly after concluding negotiations.

The Mexican consultant revealed that her biggest shock about working and negotiating with Czechs came when she realized that few Czechs feel a sense of ownership about work projects. "Once," she related, "I was asked why was I so concerned about turning a project in on time, if after all I was 'just an employee.' People thought that the boss was the person ultimately responsible for the final result and felt very little sense of accountability to the end client."

SOCIALIZING AND WORK

Once a contract has been concluded, it is customary to go out for a beer or to have a small celebration in the office. Office parties generally include Bohemian *Sekt* (Czech sparkling wine) and *chlebíčky* (small open-faced sandwiches nearly impossible to eat without gracing one's front with a pickle chunk or egg bit). At the pub, it is usual to trade drink rounds, and drinking in front of colleagues is not seen as awkward.

If you are invited out, keep talk light and limit discussions to "safe" topics. Let the Czechs determine the direction of the conversation, and don't bring up history or politics. Above all, don't be seduced into a compare-and-contrast discussion about the Czech Republic versus your home country. Those never end well.

However, if such socialization opportunities don't present themselves, it's best not to push it. Most Czechs are proud of their country, and some even like to show foreigners around after business hours, but these interactions should be initiated by your Czech colleagues. Work is not nearly as all-consuming for Czechs as it is for Americans—the motto is more "Work to Live" than "Live to Work"—and some people can be quite strict about keeping work and home life separate.

If it seems that business is being conducted at out-of-office gatherings and you feel that you might be missing out on important discussions, the best remedy is again to rely on a trustworthy local partner. It's not that all Czechs are unfriendly or unwilling to go out with foreigners, just that gaining trust inside the workplace is hard enough—gaining social trust is a much longer process and one that can be undone by a too-aggressive outsider.

chapter **nine**

COMMUNICATING

THE CZECH LANGUAGE

Czech is a difficult Slavic language with an intimidating-looking set of diacritics and more consonants than look possible in one word. It may take several days to even start to recognize common words because of how hard the language appears to be to pronounce, even though it is in Latin script.

In fact, because Czech is completely phonetic, once the basic sounds are learned, reading words and recognizing place-names (on public transportation, for example) is not difficult. The *háček* (the small "v" hook above certain letters) and *čárka* (accent mark over certain vowels) were actually introduced into the language as an attempt to simplify spelling. Without the *háčky* and *čárky* diacritics, Czech spelling would look a lot like Polish script—one of Poland's leading newspapers is the impossible-looking *Rzeczpospolita*—so the diacritics are actually a blessing.

In the case of "š," "č," and "ž," pronunciations are relatively easy for an English-speaker. The sounds are pronounced as if the letter were "sh," "ch," and "zh." A *háček* over an "e" indicates a "ye" sound. The impenetrable "ř" is the most difficult—an English speaker will probably approximate it by rolling a sort of "rzh." There are even some Czechs for whom this sound is a problem—former Czech President Václav Havel has trouble with his "ř"—so don't feel bad if you can't master it. Vowels with *čárky* will be a beat longer in duration than those without, but most non-Czech speakers will not notice the difference.

In Prague, most service workers in the center will speak at least some English, but as in most places—with the reputed exception of France—visitors' attempts to speak the language will be met warmly. (See Survival Czech below.) Outside Prague, many young people speak English, but older people are more likely to speak German.

Russian is also spoken by a large number of people because it was required during the Communist era, but many Czechs refuse to speak Russian and may even be markedly (and understandably) hostile about it. Unless it is a very important communication scenario, Russian is best not offered. (If Russian is the only other language you can speak, use it to try to pick up some Czech. The two languages are close, with some words being identical.)

Communicating in situations in which no mutual language can be found is pretty universal. Armed with a phrase book, map, and small notebook, it should be possible to get the point across. If the situation is serious, fall back on asking for an English speaker. Usually someone can be found, even if it takes a while.

Using Czech
No one expects foreigners to learn the Czech language just for a short trip. However, it will go a long way toward creating goodwill toward outsiders if you observe a few "rules" about when to offer greetings and other niceties.

When entering a shop, approaching a market stand, or having first contact with someone, it is customary to say *Dobrý den* (good day/hello). Of course, it is also possible to use good morning, good evening, and good night, but the timing is tricky and it means memorizing more phrases. *Dobrý den* works pretty well all day. When leaving, always bid the person good-bye (*na shledanou*). A "thank you" (*děkuji*) is never out of place either.

On public transportation, conditions can be crowded and contact inevitable. Using *promiňte* (excuse me) will smooth the situation. Even

pardon, pronounced with a long "o" sound and
stress on the second syllable, is better than
nothing. And if you want to find out if someone
speaks English, it's best not to launch into the
question without first saying *Dobrý den*.
Greetings are very important in the Czech
Republic, even among strangers.

SURVIVAL CZECH		
English	**Czech**	**Pronunciation**
Thank you	*Děkuju Vám*	dyeh-KOO-yoo vahm
Thanks (very informal)	*Díky*	DEE-kee
Please	*Prosím*	PROH-seem
Hello/good day	*Dobrý den!*	DOH-bree den
Good-bye	*Na shledanou*	nah-SLEH-dah-noh
Do you speak English?	*Mluvíte anglický*	MLOO-vee-teh ahn-GLEETS-kee
Excuse me/ pardon me	*Promiňte*	proh-MEEN-teh
We'd like the check, please	*Zaplatíme, prosím*	ZAH-plah-tee-meh, PROH-seem

THE PHYSICAL SIDE
The Czechs tend to be reserved in their body
language, but it's still possible to convey some
things without words. Never shy about

disapproving glances, Czechs are experts at the glower when faced with overly loud or otherwise unruly people, especially on public transportation. Conversely, if you offer your seat to an elderly person, pregnant woman, or someone with small children (as is customary and expected on public transportation), you are likely to be rewarded with a grateful smile. Failure to do so can put you back into disgusted-glare land.

One Czech habit that many visitors find disconcerting is the very common practice of staring. Where frank, interested staring would be considered highly rude in some cultures, Czechs have made it a national pastime. It could stem from the many hours that most Czechs spend on public transportation or from the relatively homogeneous culture, but whatever the reason, expect stares as a foreigner. It's easy to feel defensive or even insulted when someone stares at you, but it's not generally meant in an offensive way. If it bothers you, simply smile at the person and he or she is likely to look away almost immediately.

Unsolicited smiling brings up another point. Czechs—no matter whether on the metro, serving in a restaurant, or walking on the street—don't waste their smiles on just anyone. Many in fact see "excessive" smiling (as practiced by many North Americans, for example) as a sign of insincerity. Unless you are carrying a small baby or a dog in a bag, don't expect strangers to smile at you. It doesn't mean they are unfriendly, just that smiles are currency, and they're going to spend it when it matters. You should feel free to smile when it seems natural to you—as in most places, it can go a long way toward smoothing interactions—but if it's not reciprocated, don't be upset.

As in most European cities, the acceptable boundaries of personal space are smaller than in the U.S.A. simply because of the need to coexist in a confined space. Still, Czechs do have boundaries that should be observed, even if you feel that the expectation of personal space would be completely unrealistic on a crowded streetcar. When sitting down next to someone, be very careful never to sit on his or her jacket—move it over if you must, but expect a tongue-lashing if you sit on it.

Never put your feet on a seat or park bench, at least not in view of a *babička* (grandmother)— elderly ladies are the unofficial guardians of all that is right and proper in Czech culture. The back section of streetcars and any metro/bus area marked with a picture of a baby carriage is reserved for parents with strollers. Always make room for them. There are also official "handicapped" seats on all public transportation, and those should always be vacated for those in need, even more quickly than you would a regular seat.

COMMUNICATING WITH THE OUTSIDE WORLD

Keeping up with news of the world and friends and family at home presents no real challenge in the Czech Republic, especially in Prague. The national press is free of government interference, and international media—including cable news channels, foreign newspapers, and English-language magazines—are widely available. Even in small towns you should be able to track down an *International Herald Tribune* or a television with CNN International, if you need a fix.

Telephone

Making calls or sending e-mails home is also generally not a huge problem, although that becomes less true the farther you get from cities. Direct dialing from hotel or hostel landlines is not recommended because of bad rates and surcharges (as in most places), but pay phone cards—available at any

newsstand or anywhere else you might see the Český Telecom logo—make calling from pay phones very easy. (Český Telecom is the Czech telephone monopoly, and as such controls the rates and access to landlines and to many Internet services.)

A local or international mobile phone (such as Thuraya satellite phones) can make communication easier. The Czech Republic is on the GSM system, so any European phone will work there, but most North American phones will not. If you do have a GSM phone and are planning a longer stay, buying a local SIM card and pay-as-you-go access can save you a lot of money in roaming fees.

Internet
Accessing the Internet is a breeze in Prague. From wireless networks (usually not free) to Internet cafés, checking e-mail and using your favorite Internet sites will not present a problem. It is difficult to find free access, but most places offer fairly reasonable per-minute or per-hour charges. Hooking up a laptop can be more of a challenge unless you have wi-fi, but it is possible through some Internet cafés. Usually such facilities have an English speaker around who might be able to help.

Mail

For sending letters, packages, or postcards, you
can either buy stamps from newsstands and drop
them in one of the many orange
Česká Pošta boxes or visit the
post office. For Czechs, the post
office is not just a place to mail
things, however, so be prepared
for some confusion. At the post office, Czechs can
pay bills, bank, get insurance, fax documents,
make international calls, and so on. Each function
has its own window, and trying to get a different
service at the "wrong" window is an exercise
in futility.

At the main post office right off Wenceslas
Square (worth a visit just for its beautiful
renovation), all the functions are listed on a
machine that will spit out a number tag for
customers. The numbers then come up on
electronic signs above the windows.

Overall, the mail is quite reliable, especially
outgoing, although as in most places, sending
items of high value or cash is unadvisable. DHL,
Federal Express, and UPS all have a presence in
the Czech Republic.

CONCLUSION

Whether standing in the wrong line at the post
office or surveying the city from the mid-point of

Charles Bridge as the floodlights illuminate Prague's centuries of architecture at dusk, there is something to be learned at every turn during a visit to the Czech Republic.

For a real traveler, that learning process is what makes heading to foreign destinations special. As Gary Langer wrote in the first issue of *Transitions Abroad,* "Travelers and tourists, the distinction is simple: Tourists are those who bring their homes with them wherever they go, and apply them to whatever they see. They are closed to experiences outside of the superficial. Travelers, however, leave home at home, bringing only themselves and a desire to learn."

While not all Czechs are entirely happy that their country has become a popular tourist—and traveler—destination, they are uniformly proud of what is on offer. With a little prompting and cultural sensitivity they will be happy to share it with informed visitors. Czechs have given the world amazing gifts already—from the word "robot" to the grit and determination of distance runner and Olympic champion Emil Zatopek— and those contributions are likely to continue even as the Czech nation integrates more closely into Europe and the world.

Appendix: Some Czech Firsts

1348
The first university in central Europe was founded in Prague by Charles IV; it is still known as Charles University (Univerzita Karlova).

1411
The first Czech translation of the Bible.

1519–20
The first dollars in the world were minted at Jáchymov (in German, Joachymsthal). These were the *Joachymsthaler Gulden* (Joachymsthal florins), the name of which became shortened to *Thaler*, Czech *tolar*, then spread throughout the Habsburg lands and across the world.

1754
Prokop Diviš (1696–1765) built the first lightning conductor at Přímětice, near Znojmo. He had been working at the same time as, but independently of, Benjamin Franklin, who is also credited with the invention, the theory of which he had published in 1753.

1824–32
The first railway in continental Europe (initially horse-drawn) was constructed between Česke Budějovice and Linz by František Antonín Gerstner (1795–1840), who also built the first Russian railway, from St. Petersburg to Tsarskoye Selo.

1826
The first ship's propeller was patented by Josef Ressel, a forester of Czech descent. It was first tested on a ship in Trieste in 1829.

1827
The first modern plow that broke up the earth, as well as turning it over, was invented by the cousins František and Václav Veverka and first demonstrated at Lhota pod Libčany. Industrial manufacture began in 1849, the year the cousins died.

1865
The natural scientist and abbot of the Augustine monastery in Brno, Johann Gregor Mendel (1822–84), known as the founder of modern genetics, published his results on cross-breeding plants; he is usually accepted as an Austrian, but the Czechs are nevertheless pleased to lay some claim to him on account of where he worked.

1956
Otto Wichterle (1913–98) is credited with cocreation of hydrogels and being the main developer of the first contact lenses based on them.

1966
The first Oscar awarded to a Czech(oslovak) film was for *Shop on Main Street*.

Further Reading and Viewing

Bedford, Neal, Jane Rawson, and Matt Warren. *Lonely Planet Czech & Slovak Republics*, 4th ed. Oakland: Lonely Planet Publications, 2004.

Čapek, Karel. *Talks With T. G. Masaryk*. Translated by Dora Round. Edited by Michael Henry Heim. North Haven: Catbird Press, 1995.

Closely Watched Trains. Directed by Jiří Menzel. Prague: Barrandov Film Studios, 1967.

Hašek, Jaroslav. *The Good Soldier Švejk*. Translated and introduced by Cecil Parrott. New York: Everyman's Library, 1993.

Havel, Václav et al. *The Power of the Powerless: Citizens Against the State in Central-Eastern Europe*. Edited by John Keane. New York: M. E. Sharpe, 1990.

Hrabal, Bohumil. *I Served the King of England*. Translated by Paul Wilson. New York: Vintage International, 1990.

Jirasek, Alois. *Old Czech Legends*. Translated by Maria Holocek. London: Unesco/Forest Books, 1992.

Klima, Ivan. *The Spirit of Prague and Other Essays*. Translated by Paul Wilson. New York: Granta, 1995.

Kolya. Directed by Jan Svěrák. Prague: Biograf Jan Svěrák, Portobello Pictures, Česká televize, 1996.

Kundera, Milan. *The Book of Laughter and Forgetting*. Translated from the French by Aaron Asher. New York: HarperPerennial, 1996.

Little Otik. Directed by Jan Svankmajer. Prague: Zeitgeist Films Ltd., 2000.

Pekárková, Iva. *Truck Stop Rainbows*. Translated by David Powelstock. New York: Farrar, Straus & Giroux, 1992.

Tizard, Will. *Time Out Prague*, 6th edition. London: Time Out, 2004.

Index

Acknowledgments

I am indebted to the numerous Czechs and expatriates who have shared
their knowledge of and experiences in the Czech Republic with me, and in
particular to Iain Alexander, Beatriz Castillo, and Trey Vincent for their
extensive assistance with the business chapter. This book would not have
been possible without the adventurous spirit of Chip Ritter, who left
everything safe and English-speaking so we could move to Prague together.
Thanks also to my parents, Carl and Pat Rosenleaf, for understanding my
                                        to